Coping with the Family

PETER COREY

Illustrated by Martin Brown

Hippo

Scholastic Children's Books,
Scholastic Publications Ltd,
7–9 Pratt Street, London NW1 0AE, UK

Scholastic Inc.,
555 Broadway, New York, NY 10012–3999, USA

Scholastic Canada Ltd,
123 Newkirk Road, Richmond Hill,
Ontario, Canada L4C 3G5

Ashton Scholastic Pty Ltd,
PO Box 579, Gosford, New South Wales,
Australia

Ashton Scholastic Ltd,
Private Bag 92801, Penrose, Auckland,
New Zealand

First published by Scholastic Publications Ltd, 1994

ISBN 0 590 55524 3

Printed by Cox and Wyman Ltd, Reading, Berks

10 9 8 7 6 5 4 3 2 1

Contents

Dedication

To all branches of my family everywhere: the Coreys, the Cooks, the Flippances, the Morgans, the Chares, Evenses, Joneses (they take some keeping up with!), the Coopers and the Beatties – not to mention the ones I don't know about. Well, I can't really mention them if I don't know about them, can I?

Acknowledgement

The famous naturalist and novelist, Gerald Durrell, once wrote a brilliant book called *My Family And Other Animals*. I've never read it.

Peter Corey

Foreword ...

Everybody's got one. Some people have got really big ones. Some have got very small ones. Some people have lost theirs, often through no fault of their own. Some think they've never had one, but then discover that they've probably had quite a decent-sized one for years without realising it. Some people lose theirs, then find another one and quite often the new one is better than the one they had in the first place. Some people think that other people's are better than theirs, but if they were to swap they'd probably find that there's hardly any difference at all. What am I talking about? The mind boggles! Unless of course you read the title of this book. Then you'll know exactly what I'm on about. That's right! Families! Of course if you didn't read the title,

then your mind has probably been doing overtime trying to work out what I was referring to. Good! At least I've got your attention! So now I suggest that you read on – as long as you've paid for the book!

Families: The Problem Identified

Nothing is certain in life. Oh, apart from the fact that we're all going to die some day, England are never going to win at cricket and I'm never going to be able to teach my dog to juggle.[1] Oh, and the other big certainty is that you're never going to be able to choose your relatives. When you're born you have absolutely no say in who your Mum and Dad are going to be.[2] You're too young to understand, for a start. If you weren't – if, for instance, babies were born with the brain and capabilities of, say, a ten-year-old – you might take one look at your loving parents and bribe the nurse to switch name tags with the kid in the next cot. Not that his parents

IF YOU'LL SWAP ME YOUR FAMILY FOR MY FAMILY I'LL THROW IN THIS TWINKLY-DINKLY MOBILE

IT'S A DEAL

1. But, like the England cricket team, I'm not giving up!
2. Or brother and sister for that matter, which is what makes the situation all the more desperate!

look much better than yours, but at least they look like they might have a bit of cash, which could make all that stupid *coochy coochy cooing* almost bearable. Don't be fooled. All the money in the world wouldn't make any difference.

Families are families are families. They all contain the same hideous jumble of social and intellectual misfits, cunningly mix 'n' matched to make everyone else's family look more attractive than yours. This is one of the cruellest facts about them. For some reason, other people's families look quite normal until you become involved with them. Then you realise they're just the same as yours, only switched around a bit. Take a look at the Johnstones up the road. OK, so their dad doesn't shout as much as yours, but then they've got an Uncle Reg who's a part-time Mad Axeman. They've got a poodle, whereas you've got a pit-bull. Well, they don't need a pit-bull – their little boy Kevin bites the postman at their house.

THANK YOU SO MUCH. THIS ANKLE-BITING BIT JUST ISN'T ME

GRRRRR

The same thing happens when you get married. Yes, I realise that that's not likely to happen for – ooh, at least a fortnight yet,[1] but it's best to be forewarned. Well, you know what they say: forewarned is forearmed.[2] And this is why I've covered the subject in some detail – later in the book.

However, we needn't concern ourselves with marrying into other people's families just yet. With any luck, by the time you're old enough to be thinking about doing it, you'll have learned to cope with your own family. Because that's what this book is all about – coping with the family. Hence the rather snappy title! I could have called it *The Idiot's Guide to Bulgarian-Rules Football*, but that would only have been confusing, as there will probably be little or no information about Bulgarian-rules football between the pages of this particular tome, even the kind of stuff that would appeal to idiots.[3] But let's focus on the here-and-now. Your present family.

1. Mainly because marriage interferes with your homework.
2. Who says that? And where do the other two arms come from?
3. Although there might be – who knows?

Problems: The Family Identified

Just for the sake of argument, let's pretend that you're a typical young person. Can you imagine that? Let's pretend – also for the sake of argument – that you're called Shane (or Sharon). Okay? Can you handle that? Do you need a few minutes to get used to the idea? Well, you can't have them. We haven't got time.

Right now, Shane/Sharon. Close your eyes and listen to the noises around you. If what you can hear is a perfectly intelligible conversation containing no reference to string, the cat's boil or the neighbours' woodlouse collection, then what you can hear is probably the television set. If, on the other hand, what you can hear is an apparently disconnected jumble of words which have no common theme, make no sense and have almost certainly been made up, then you're probably sitting in the bosom of your family.[1] Now open your eyes and look around. If the room is filled with a strange collection of misfits who would only ever come together for some sort of stunt set up for *Noel's House Party*, then this should confirm that you're at home with the rest of your tribe. If further confirmation is required, try saying, "Mum?" or "Dad?". If you get no reply, except possibly a grunt, then that is positive proof that you're at home with your kith and kin.[2]

---

1. If everything seems muffled, as though you're under water, then you're probably sitting in the bosom of your Great Aunt Doris, and I suggest you move pretty sharpish before she starts measuring you up for a cardigan!
2. You might even be at home with your Keith and Ken, if indeed any of your family have been lumbered with these unfortunate names.

Look at them – if you can bear to. The newspaper going up and down in time to the horribly loud snoring noise is Dad – your father. If you're male, you may even be his son and heir, which means that one day you'll inherit all you now see: the pot belly, the fatigue, the record-breaking snoring, even the newspaper. Not that daughters get off scot-free. Oh, no!

Now look around, in the general direction of that tutting noise. Yes. The woman staring at the TV and tutting is Mum. She's not a TV critic – far from it. Anyway, what would be the point? She's watching *Home and Away*. No, the reason she's tutting is because

none of the mums in *Home and Away* behave like real people. They never rumple their child's hair when he or she has just spent two hours grooming it prior to going out on a heavy date. They never embarrass their off-spring in front of their classmates by insisting that they clean out the gerbil. And they *never* discuss intimate personal matters, such as "Have you still got that spot on your bottom? Can I see it?" Oh, no! Mums in soap operas never behave like that. And do you know why? I'll tell you. It's because soap operas are written by people with families, and they know that real-life families are far too hideous to put on TV.

Take another look around. If you can see somebody apparently performing an operation on a Yorkshire terrier, that's probably your little brother. The operation is something to do with homework. I think it's called "avoiding doing homework", actually. The big drippy girl wearing far too much perfume and staring out of the window as though she'd been mesmerised several years earlier by a very bad stage hypnotist (who then forgot how to reverse the process) is probably your big sister. She's waiting for her boyfriend to turn up, although it's looking as though he's forgotten. Let's face it, she *is* quite forgettable. Still, he seems to like her. But then he's not much better himself, come to think of it. Not that you *do* think about it that much. Your big sister's love life is of no interest to you. Or at least it wouldn't be, but for the fact that the minute the boyfriend is spotted coming up the garden path, you're all rounded up and locked in the airing cupboard.

Oh, I almost forgot. That little bundle of woollens is Granny. She hasn't spoken to you since you tried to get 50p for her from the Oxfam shop. It wasn't so much that she minded being sold – she's always encouraged you to be enterprising. But she didn't take kindly to you saying "Okay" when the assistant said: "I can only give you 25p, and even then I'm robbing myself". She's funny like that.

Unlike Grandad. Did he ever complain

about being driven around the streets in an old pram, trick or treating for Hallowe'en? No. He was a real sport. He didn't even want a cut of the takings. Not that you made much money – he tended to frighten people off until you splashed out on the witch's mask for him. You did better in the few weeks leading up to Bonfire Night, but then he disappeared. It was funny, that. Well, maybe funny's an odd choice of word, but it was certainly strange. You only left him parked by a well-stacked but unlit bonfire for an hour while you went and bought some fireworks, and when you came back, he'd gone.

According to your Uncle Kenny, he was abducted by aliens. And he should know. He's got all the *Star Trek* films on video and the walls of his room at the daycare centre are lined with tin foil. What he doesn't know about aliens isn't worth knowing, apparently. But a couple of things about that night still puzzle you:

1 Why should aliens be interested in your grandad? After all, nobody else was. Not even your grandma.

2 Why should aliens want to abduct the bonfire as well? What possible use would they have for it? But they did. When you got back from the paper shop with your box of fireworks,[1] it had all gone – Grandad, bonfire, the lot.[2] All that was left was a big charred circle. That's what happens when alien spaceships take off, according to Uncle Kenny.

Of course the police weren't interested. They didn't believe the alien theory for a minute. They reckoned it looked as though someone had set fire to the bonfire as a prank. Which didn't really explain your grandad's disappearance.

As for your Auntie Beryl, she's a medium. Well, she was, but she's put on a bit of weight since she joined *Fat Watchers*, so she's more of an extra-large now. But she does predict the future with tarot cards. Well, *playing* cards, anyway. Well, she was once playing poker during the post-Christmas dinner lull before the Queen's speech, and she predicted that Uncle Geoff was going to lose a fortune. This had less to do with her card-reading skill and more to do with the fact that Geoff had just bet all his money and she knew she had all four aces in her hand,[3] but it still gave her a totally undeserved reputation as a spiritualist.

---

1. A Bumper Assortment with all the pretty ones taken out and a few extra-bangy ones put in.
2. Even the mask, which you'd borrowed from Derek Template and had to give him 50p for because he threatened to tell his big brother who eats people (but only for fun, it's not his proper job).
3. A pretty good hand in any game, except possibly table tennis.

Consequently, it was Auntie Beryl who was called upon to try and contact Grandad in whatever galaxy he now resided. However, all Beryl's attempts so far have failed miserably. According to Uncle Kenny, this is entirely due to aliens blocking the inter-galactic thought-routes, whatever they are. The rest of us know that the real reason why she's failed to contact Grandad in his new stellar sheltered housing complex is because, like Kenny, Beryl is completely mad. But who's going to tell her? Certainly not your mum, because if she did, who would she get to wax her legs in future?

So this is your family. Well, your family for the sake of argument, anyway. Although they probably do feel vaguely familiar. This is because all families are basically the same – it's just that names have been changed to protect the innocent and the criminally insane.[1] But how do families get the way they are? Is it pure fluke that each one gets its fair share of lunatics, geniuses and train-spotters? Is this part of some great Master Plan, some scheme to share out the weirdos, so that they don't all wind up at the same family events? Well, to try and answer this, we need to go right back to the beginning. So let's do that.[2]

1. Yes! Just what was Second Cousin Damien doing with four hundredweight of assorted dog biscuits at Our Tracey's wedding?
2. No, no! I don't mean right back to the beginning of the book! What's the matter with you? Are there any more like you in your house? I do hope not!

In The Beginning......

If Darwin's theory of evolution is to be believed, all humans are descended from apes. Well, we probably all know somebody who looks as though they might be, but consider this theory carefully. Apes, in their natural habitat,[1] sit around eating and scratching their bottoms. They seem to get along with the rest of their family, unless someone tries to pinch their lunch, when they have a bit of a punch-up. All of which seems perfectly reasonable to me, and is enough to convince me that we cannot possibly be descended from them (although the bottom-scratching bit sounds familiar). Or any other animal for that matter. So . . . nice try, Darwin, but I think you're talking through your hat, if you're wearing one.

But what about God? Personally I don't have any quarrel with the idea that Man and Woman were created by a God. And I think He (or She) didn't do too badly, considering that it was a bit of a rush job. You see, humans are fine, individually. It's when they get

1. Which is *not* a zoo, incidentally.

together in groups that the trouble starts. Not that there's anything new or original in that. History is littered with the debris of broken families. Let's take a look at . . .

☞Relative Histories☜

From the moment that prehistoric Uncle Ugg clipped his young nephew Igg round the earhole, just because Igg had poked Ugg's pet mammoth with a pointed stick, families have been at each other's throats. Now, since you won't find this family feud particularly well documented in school history books, perhaps I should tell you about it, just in case you ever get a question about it in some future exam. After Ugg had thumped Igg, Igg's dad (Egg) called Ugg an Agg-Agg (which was apparently very, very rude in those days) and flatly refused to teach him to do those clever little twiddly bits on cave paintings, or go hunting with him. Ugg stormed off in a huff[1] and they didn't speak again from that day to this. Or rather they didn't speak again from that day until the day they all died.[2] Not that they spoke much even before they stopped talking to each other, unless of course you count going "Ugg!"

1. Which is in fact what huffs were called in those days. *Huff* is one of the few prehistoric words that still survive today. *Egg* is another, although in those days it didn't mean "white and yellow thing that chickens lay for breakfast", but was an early form of the name Kevin.
2. This day was a Thursday. They all got eaten by the mammoth, who had become very sulky and unpredictable since people stopped poking him with sticks, which was his favourite game.

This is just one example of the way that relatives and families interact. History is, of course, full of such examples. You don't have to go back as far as ancient Egypt to find family strife.

Cleopatra gets the Needle

Ptolemy V, King of Egypt, had two children: Ptolemy Junior (later called Ptolemy VI) and his older sister Cleopatra (later still called Cleopatra). Unfortunately, they fell out. This won't seem particularly unusual to you, especially if you've got a younger brother (or older sister). One can only imagine what the fight was about. History tells us that it was about neither of them wanting to rule alongside the other. So what did they do? Moan to their mum? Well, I don't know about that because my history book doesn't mention their mum at all. So maybe they complained to their dad? Difficult, since he was dead and that was why they had become joint rulers in the first place. I'll tell you what they did, shall I? They had a fight.

Now, we're not talking about your typical brother/sister spat here – angry words, thrown gerbils, that sort of thing. Oh, no! We're talking war. Yes! They both got armies together[1] and fought it out. Cleo cheated a bit, probably because she was losing. She phoned Rome – or at least sent a carrier pigeon – to her friend and admirer Julius Caesar, the nobbliest Roman of them all (particularly his knees). The message read: "Cannot ptolerate Ptolemy any more. Ptolemy needs pting to death". Which is what happened. There was a huge battle, the result of which was: Romans 1 – Ptolemy lost. After that

1. Which was easy enough because obviously they both had a bob or two, being royalty.

Cleopatra ruled alone, until she had that nasty accident with the snake. Now don't let this give you any ideas. Don't go phoning the parachute regiment just because you and your brother can't decide who should eat the last yoghurt.

Hannibal Packs his Trunk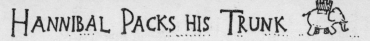

Not that all family rows are to do with sibling rivalry. Take Hannibal, for instance. We all know that he made a famous Alpine crossing, accompanied by a herd of pachyderms. What is very rarely reported in history books is the fact that, as he left home, his wife yelled after him (as she bounced his suitcase off the back of his head), "And take those bloomin' elephants with you!" You see, something that has always been regarded as a feat of endurance was in fact caused by a lovers' tiff.

BOO-HOO-OUDICCA

Mind you, history is stuffed full of that kind of thing. Take Boudicca for instance. Whether you call her Boudicca or Boadicea, we all know that she was the Celtic Queen who fought the Romans and cut them down to size.[1] What you probably don't know is why. (Until now, because now I'm going to tell you.) It was all to do with her *Old Man*. Now, by *Old Man* I mean husband. However, Boudicca's husband was also a genuine old man. How old? How should I know? But old, anyway. His name was Prasutagus, so I would imagine he was pretty grumpy too. Well, wouldn't you be with a name like that? Anyway, before he died he wrote a will,[2] leaving half his kingdom[3] to Emperor Nero, the well-known Roman violinist and arsonist, and the rest to his two daughters. Boudicca got nothing.[4]

She wasn't happy, I can tell you! She wasn't the jolliest person at the best of times[5] and, as we already know, she did have a bit of a temper. However, she played the dutiful widow. At the gathering after the funeral she moved among the mourners with trays of individual pork pies and spam sandwiches with the crusts cut off, making light conversation and listening to numerous elderly relatives, who she never saw from one year's end to the next, going on about how Prasutagus had always promised them his ornamental spittoon.

1. Which isn't difficult when you've got huge blades attached to your chariot wheels.
2. Obviously he did it *before* he died, not after!
3. His kingdom was in fact Norfolk, but it was called something else in those days.
4. Well, nothing apart from a couple of campaign medals and some rabbit-bone cufflinks.
5. In fact she only knew one joke. It was about a Celt, a Pict and a Scot having a game of cricket. She rarely told it because it never got a laugh. This had a little to do with her comic delivery, and a lot to do with the fact that no-one understood it, because cricket hadn't been invented then.

Then Nero, who always had appalling timing,[1] turned up to claim his inheritance. Well, naturally he didn't actually turn up himself. He sent a messenger[2] with a tape measure. Tactless or what? But while the messenger was making an inventory of the silver and wrestling with a maiden aunt who was trying to make off with a particularly attractive figurine of a stuck pig, Boudicca decided to take her revenge on the Romans. She went on the rampage, and chased the Romans from London to Colchester and Verulamium.[3] The rest is history.

1. Who else would organise a violin recital on the same night that Rome burned to the ground?
2. Being a messenger was a lousy job in those days. Mainly because all messengers were marked *Read and Destroy* and for centuries people thought this instruction referred to the messenger, not the message.
3. Which is now called St Albans, which must please the Post Office.

History books don't say why Prasutagus should have left his wife out of his will. Obviously it had something to do with a domestic tiff. It always does. Maybe she squeezed the toothpaste from the middle or something. Who knows? The historians obviously didn't think it was worth finding out.

Will's Will

Similarly, no-one has explained why that most famous of all playwrights, William Shakespeare, should only leave his wife, Anne Hathaway, the "second-best bed" in his will. However, what I can tell you is that the bed wasn't his to bequeath. It already belonged to Anne. She had brought it with her when they got married. So William was insulting her twice over by giving her something she already owned! But then – that's families for you! And Royalty are every bit as bad! For example . . .

UNCIVIL WAR

Henry I nominated his daughter Matilda as his successor. But after his death, when he was too stiff to do anything about it, the Royal Council decided that they didn't fancy Matilda as Queen. Why, I don't know. But it could have had something to do with the fact that Henry had also proclaimed that the National Anthem should be changed to *Waltzing Matilda*.[1] Anyway, the Council chose William the Conqueror's son Stephen.

1. Up until then the National Anthem was *Henry's a Jolly Good Fellow (And So Say All Of Us)*.

Have you ever heard of King Steve? Of course not! Because he only reigned for a year.[1] Taking a leaf from Cleopatra's book, Matilda got an army together and waged a civil war against Steve's lot. This went on for eight years.[2] Eventually Matilda decided that she didn't fancy being queen after all – the crown was heavy, it wasn't her colour, etc. So she agreed that Steve could be king as long as her son Henry II could succeed him. Steve agreed, which was handy because he died a year later and Henry came to the throne.[3] But the Royal Family feuding continued.

DO YOU LIKE YOUR NEW CROWN STEVE? I DESIGNED IT MYSELF

GEE THANKS MATILDA

Lion Bars are on Me

When Henry II's son Richard the Lionheart[4] went to the Crusades, what did his brother John do? Send him food parcels? Cash? Postcards? Not on your life! He took over England and ruled it into the ground. If it hadn't been for Kevin Costner swinging through trees in green tights, there might not be a Great Britain today. Good old Kevin, I say.[5]

1. More of a short shower really!
2. Mainly because she didn't have the Romans on her side. They'd all died out long before.
3. He was 14, so there's hope for you yet (as long as you're under 14)! Incidentally he was known as Henry Plantagenet, because he wore a sprig of broom in his hat. Work that one out if you can!
4. Not called Lionheart because he had a lion's heart in his hat, by the way!
5. Or was it Robin Hood?

HENRY VIII & CO.

Then of course there was good old Henry VIII who, when he wasn't writing folk songs,[1] went around chopping his wives' heads off. Then there was his daughter Elizabeth I: thrown into the tower by her half-sister Mary, Elizabeth later had her Scottish cousin's (also called Mary) head chopped off.

But what about the lesser-known relatives of history? The ones who didn't make it into the papers? Well, the pages of history are covered in the unpleasant stains left behind by these people. But who were they? My team of highly motivated but lowly paid researchers scoured the four corners of the Scunthorpe Public Library and Turkish Baths Complex,[2] and came up with the following:

1. *Greensleeves* was one of his. *God Save The Queen* wasn't!
2. Actually Turkish Baths are very complex. I don't know if you've ever had one.

Great Relatives From History

It's a little known fact that Ivan the Terrible had a brother. All most history books say about him is that Ivan had a big sword which he kept sticking into people. They never mention the fact that he had a brother as well. But he did – Les-The-Quite-Pleasant-Really-When-You-Get-To-Know-Him. Most people called him "Oi! Fatso!" Not that Les minded. Unlike his brother. Why, you couldn't even smile at Ivan across the dinner table without suddenly finding one of your ears floating in your soup.

Les was a bit more of a diplomat. Well, somebody had to be. Ivan was rapidly giving the family a bad name, so Les took it upon himself to limit the damage being done to their reputation by quietly telling people that Ivan didn't really mean it, he was just being playful. Of course it wasn't always easy. I mean it's quite difficult to persuade someone who's just had their head lopped off and skewered onto a pole that it was just a bit of fun. For a start, which half of the body do you tell?

As you might imagine, Ivan didn't appreciate the efforts his brother was making on his behalf. (Do they ever?) In fact, Les's diplomacy was finally his undoing. He was just trying to persuade a lone Macedonian that his entire village had been massacred and all the buildings razed to the ground "as a joke" when Ivan overheard him and said "Are you whispering about me?" Before Les could reply, his head was sitting on the floor looking up at the rest of his body with a "what did I say?" expression on its face. Oh well, you could never acccuse Ivan of nepotism.[1]

---

1. Even if you knew what it meant.

27

Michelangelo would not be famous today[1] if it weren't for his cousin Phil Angelo. For it was Phil who pointed out that before you paint something it needs an undercoat. Oh, yes! He may have dribbled, mumbled to himself a lot and worn his coat back to front, but he knew a thing or two about decorating, did Phil! If it hadn't been for Phil, all those years painting the ceiling of the Sistine Chapel would have been wasted, because without an undercoat the paint would have soaked into the ceiling and disappeared. Good old Phil! Without him the Sistine Chapel would not be the marvel it is today.[2] The paint would have flaked and the Pope would have got somebody in to coat it with artex swirls. Oh, lovely![3]

Then of course there was Lucrezia Borgia's sister Cheryl. Lucrezia may have been a great Renaissance poisoner, but Cheryl was the real cook of the family. Why, she could make a curry that would take the roof off your mouth! Of course, if Lucrezia managed to get at it, you'd hardly notice the heat. You'd be far too busy rolling around the floor, clutching your throat and

1. What d'you mean, you've never heard of him?
2. Incidentally it was also Phil who persuaded Michelangelo to paint out the *Scrabble* board, since there is absolutely no evidence to suggest that they played *Scrabble* at the Last Supper.
3. Whoever thought of artex swirls? And why didn't one of their relatives shoot them?

BELIEVE ME MICK, IT NEEDS A SECOND COAT

dying. Ironically, this is how Lucrezia's poisoning activities went undetected for so long. Everyone assumed that people were dying because they weren't used to spicy food.[1]

And let's not forget Saint Francis of Assisi's cousin Geoff, who had a thriving poultry business. Well, maybe thriving is a slight exaggeration. Actually, he wandered the streets with a couple of sparrows tied to a stick, but only because he was mad. He would accost anyone prepared to listen and tell them all about his famous relative. "I remember when he was called Frank," he would tell them. The thing that annoyed him most was the fact that Saint F. hardly acknowledged him. Not that you could blame him. Because having a lunatic for a cousin can seriously affect your credibility,[2] let alone your chances of becoming a saint.

Good man though he undoubtedly was, Saint Francis could easily have been the sort of person about whom people said: "Frank who?" And all because of his cousin. Just as Saint Crispin could have gone into the plastic beach flip-flop business and lost out on becoming the Patron Saint of Cobblers if he'd listened to his twin sister Dawn. You see, ever since the beginning of time, family ties have bound and gagged the great and good as

1. At the time this was referred to as *Death by Vindaloo*.
2. Believe me, I know!

well as the poor and feeble-minded, and it's only because of their greatness (or madness) that they've survived at all, let alone achieved fame.

Of course having relatives isn't always a bad thing, though most of the time it is. Take Lot, for instance. If his Uncle Wilf hadn't said: "Don't look now, but your wife's just turned into a pillar of salt", he might have suffered the same fate. But these examples of family loyalty are rare. Mostly families are something to be endured rather than cherished. And that's as true today as it was when Man was just a monkey having a shave.[1]

IT WAS WHILE VISITING THE GALAPAGOS ISLANDS THAT I BEGAN TO SEE HOW EVOLUTION MIGHT WORK

DARWIN TALKING THROUGH HIS HAT

1. According to Darwin.

Let Bygones Be Bygones

Having said all this, perhaps we shouldn't be searching through history for the answer to the problem of how to cope with the family. Although it's reassuring to know that the problem has been in existence since the beginning of time, I think we ought to concern ourselves with the here-and-now. After all, Lucrezia Borgia isn't likely to bother you, is she! What we should actually be doing is confronting the problem head-on. Some great general once said (probably just before he got shot accidentally by his own men), "In order to defeat him, you must first know your enemy." Well, that's what we must do now. We must consider relatives individually and find out what makes them tick and how long they tick before they explode.

In order to do this we must divide them up. Pass the scalpel! (Only joking.) I mean divide them into types, which may make them easier to observe. It may not make them any easier to handle, but it'll certainly help us to examine them. To help do this, I have provided this easy-reference Family Tree.

GRANDFATHER

ELDERLY AUNT

GRAND-MOTHER

LONG LOST RELATIVE

AUNT

AUNT   UNCLE

OLDER SISTER

COUSINS

A Relatively Simple A-Z...

Coping with the family can be as tricky as walking through a minefield wearing Arnie Schwarzenegger's boots.[1] Mainly because there are so many of them.[2] You may think you have a small family, but do something unusual like winning the Pools and you'll soon discover that you have a small army of grannies, grandpas, aunties, uncles, neighbours who call themselves "Auntie" (or "Uncle"), distant cousins, cousins who live just around the corner, cousins once removed, cousins once removed and then put back again, cousins twice removed or even mislaid completely, that you never even knew about! But that's where this section of the book will come in handy. Over the next pages you will find most of the relative types that you're likely to encounter, plus a few that I hope you never will! I've arranged them in easy-to-follow alphabetical order.

Type Name Brother, Uncle, Aunt, Father, etc.

Relationship Exactly how they are related to you and the rest of your family.

Habitat Where you're most likely to bump into them.

Behaviour Some of the embarrassing and/or weird things they get up to.

Catch phrase Most relatives have a catch phrase. This is often the only way of spotting them. Learn these and watch out for them. It could save you a lot of hassle!

Avoidance tactics A few suggested ways to avoid suffering from the particular relative's behaviour.

Other advice (where applicable). Other advice, really!

Those are the categories. This is the A – Z . . .

1. I'm assuming of course that Arnie wears boots the size of Wimbledon. The point I'm trying to make is that coping with the family is very, very tricky indeed, OK?
2. The family, that is – not Arnie's boots. I mean, whatever else he may have that the rest of us don't, he's still only got two feet.

Aunt...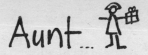

Relationship

Anyone who is a sister to either your father or your mother is an aunt. Anyone who isn't aren't. Er . . . sorry! I mean isn't. Oh, you know what I mean! Anyway, basically your mum and dad's sister(s) is (are) aunts. If that sounds complicated, the simplest thing to remember is this: aunts are sisters. This should explain everything.

Habitat

There was a time when families lived very close to each other. As the children of the family grew up, got married, had children and started looking for their own house, they tended not to move too far away from their mums and dads. So you would often only have to go next door to find your auntie. This could be seen as a good or bad thing, depending on who you were. As travel became easier, more people got cars, British Rail replaced the horses pulling their trains with engines, etc., families started to live further apart. Because of this, many people only see their aunts at family occasions (*see* Births, Deaths, Marriages and Fights). Again, this can be a good or bad thing (usually bad)!

Behaviour

As I said earlier, aunts are sisters. So if you've got a sister or have been reading up about them because you're thinking of getting one, you'll understand exactly what

I'm saying: sisters are trouble! That may seem like an outrageous sweeping generalisation, but it's true. Without exception all sisters are trouble.

Who fed your hamster while you were away on the school trip? That's right – your sister! Now, you would have thought that even a sister could understand a simple instruction like "Please feed my hamster," wouldn't you? And to be fair she did feed it, in a way. She fed it to the next-door's cat! And just two weeks away from the final of *Starpets* too! It had taken you weeks to teach it to juggle as well! OK, you got your own back. Do you remember her first boyfriend? The one with the spots? (Well, they all had spots, but this one's face looked like the surface of the moon.) Do you remember what you did? That's right! You hid all your school mates in the sideboard, and charged them £1 a head to watch your sister on the sofa (through holes you'd drilled in the door).[1]

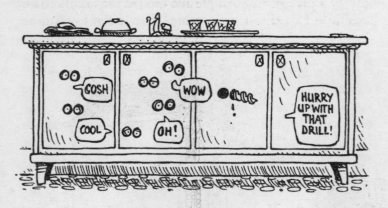

1. It wasn't worth it at all. Your dad took the money from you to pay for the damage to the door. But that wasn't the end of it, was it? A couple of years later, when you started having sex education lessons at school, all those kids came back to you for a refund, because they now realised that what they'd paid a pound to watch wasn't a couple in the throes of passion, but two teenagers playing *Twister*.

That was a mistake, which you will pay for in later life, because one day that sister may grow up into an aunt.[1] And then she'll get revenge for all those little (and big) things you did to her as a child. But she'll be subtle(ish). She won't actually do anything to you, but she will get at you through your children. Think about it.

Think about your own auntie. Think back to that Christmas when you were four. Do you remember that really noisy machine gun that lit up and threw out sparks? The one that gave your father a thumping headache and set fire to the living-room curtains? Brilliant, wasn't it? You were the only kid in the street to get a personal visit from the fire brigade that Christmas morning, without having to give a donation to charity. It was doubly brilliant because all the firemen were dressed up as Santa's elves. It was the best Christmas treat ever, wasn't it? Well, who bought you that gun that sparked off (literally) all that trouble and caused the family to not talk to each other for six years? That's right – Auntie! Your dad's sister! 'Nuff said, I think!

1. Well, *grow up* is just a figure of speech, because even a basic knowledge of adults will tell you that they never actually grow up. They just get taller.

Catch Phrase

These are various, but the one to watch out for is *Don't worry. I'll have a word with your dad!* This usually happens just after you've mentioned (quite casually) that your dad won't let you do something – go to Melanie Fishpaste's birthday disco with your best mate Tracy, have a mountain bike, move to the Bahamas, that sort of thing. You're not even bothered. You know you were trying it on, and you weren't at all surprised when Dad foamed at the mouth and said "Over my dead body!" because that's how he always reacts. Imagine your amazement when, after only a very short conversation with your aunt,[1] your dad comes into the room with two tickets for a mountain-biking holiday in the Bahamas, and suggests that you take Tracy with you. OK, so he says it through gritted teeth and Auntie's standing in the shadows, but he says it.

Avoidance Tactics...

Well, aunts don't always need avoiding. It rather depends on what they're like. At best they can be real allies. At worst, however, they can be complete pains (*see below*).

Other Advice

Before you get too carried away with thinking what a wonderful person your auntie is and how could you be so lucky as to be related to such a paragon, etc., etc., just remember: like all average humans, she's another side and, given the right environment, you'll see it soon enough! (*See also* section on Weddings.)

1. A conversation you couldn't hear properly, even with a glass pressed to the wall.

Aunt (Elderly)

There is a point at which aunts stop being allies and start being trouble, although it doesn't always happen. I have to say that I've always enjoyed the best of friendships with my aunts.[1] But some aunts are always trouble, even though they mean well. These aunts are usually elderly, and are probably not proper aunties at all. So just who are these charlatans?

Relationship

Well, of course they're not really charlatans at all, although it is possible for them to be complete strangers who wandered in during some family gathering and have been there ever since. But assuming that this isn't the case, just who are these elderly aunts? Well, if they're elderly, it's very likely that they aren't your father's or mother's sisters. They may well be your grandparents' sisters, which makes them great-aunts, but they're still referred to as aunties. The only thing that sets them apart from real aunties is . . . wool.

Habitat

They are only to be found in two places: wool shops[2] or large, comfortable, over-stuffed armchairs.[3] They never seem to need to get up and go to the toilet. Even if they

1. I have to say that, in case they gang up on me and remove bits of my body!
2. It's unlikely that you will ever *see* them in a wool shop, since they like to buy their wool in private. I'm convinced there's a secret society of knitters, and anyone entering a wool shop unannounced would be treated to secret signals, rolled-down stockings and complicated ritualistic dancing involving several assorted knitting needles.
3. It's also very unlikely that the armchair was actually that shape before the auntie sat in it. The over-stuffing is largely due to the aunt!

did, they wouldn't tell you about it. They belong to an era when things like going to the toilet weren't discussed in public. They also never eat, because they wouldn't want to dribble on the knitting. Also they've usually mislaid their teeth.

Behaviour

Always very friendly. Very, very friendly. Smotheringly friendly. In fact their cardigans[1] work rather like a magnetic 3-ply black hole, so never stand too close. If you do, at best you'll be fitted for a Winnie the Pooh tanktop, and at worst you'll be sucked in, never to be seen again.

Catch Phrase

There are several, all of which spell trouble of one kind or another. The most popular are:

Looks like I'm going to have to start a new ball. This is an old knitting expression, apparently. It can be misinterpreted, however, which is probably why no elderly aunt has ever become a Wimbledon umpire.

Let's try the sleeve. Another knitting expression, designed to get you to show an interest in the garment she's knitting. You may think "Well it's not for me. What harm can it do if I just stand there while she checks the length of the sleeve?" However, if you take a close look you'll quickly realise that it isn't for anybody. (Not unless they're two foot six tall with seven legs, anyway.) This is because she's not actually knitting anything for anyone. She's gathering victims. If you show too much interest in checking the sleeve, the next thing you know

1. Self-knitted, naturally.

you'll be presented with some ghastly garment that you'll be expected to wear every time she visits the house from now until the day you die. But – you're probably saying – if you never see the finished product of all the knitting she does in her chair, how come the ghastly sweater she makes for you appears in about 24 hours? Simple. She does it at home. On a machine.

Anyone seen my teeth? means she's hungry.

Ouch! My bum! means she's found her teeth.

Avoidance Tactics...

It's very hard to avoid this kind of relative without being rude. So be rude. "I'm not wearing that!" does it every time!

Other Advice

Don't imagine that just because this auntie is millions of years older than you, there'll come a day when she will ("sadly") no longer be around. She has been cloned. Many, many times over!

HELLO, I'M YOUR AUNTIE MABEL

Brother

Although brothers come in all shapes, sizes and colours, they tend to fall into two categories: older brothers and younger brothers. Scratch the surface of anyone's older brother, and you'll discover that they are basically the same animal as your own older brother. Hose the mud off a younger brother and the same would be true. Therefore I have divided this category into two groups. You'll find them under Older Brothers, for older brothers, and Younger Brothers for younger brothers. This only took me a few hours to work out, and I think it's rather clever!

Cousin

The main thing to remember about this species is that they are usually somebody's brother or sister, although they don't have to be. I mention this because it may go part of the way to explaining their behaviour. It may, but I doubt it!

Relationship

A cousin can be either male or female. Rarely both, although it's not impossible. Normally speaking,[1] a cousin is the child of either your mother's sister or brother, or your father's sister or brother. Rarely both, although again this is not impossible.

1. Although it's quite hard to speak normally about a cousin.

Habitat

In the old days[1] families tended to live near each other, as I think I've already mentioned. This often meant that you lived only a few doors away from aunts, uncles, etc. Now, although this might seem like a good idea, given that uncles and aunts can be very supportive, this won't necessarily hold true for their children – your cousins. There's an old Chinese expression . . . but I won't bore you with it now because it has absolutely no bearing on what we're talking about. There is however a theory that suggests that cousins who live near each other become like brothers or sisters. And that's the problem.

Behaviour

OK, so maybe cousins don't try to get into the bathroom when you're doing those little embarrassing things that little brothers can always be guaranteed to walk in on, even if it means breaking the lock. But in every other way they can be relied upon to resort to the worst excesses of brotherly/sisterly behaviour. What's more, being a member of another branch of your family, they can spread your discomfort further afield. So if you want the entire family to know about your boil, tell a cousin![2]

1. When Cliff Richard was younger.
2. Actually, sometimes it's a good idea for the family to know about your physical problems. Especially if an elderly aunt is knitting you a tank-top.

Catch Phrase

The one to be very careful of is *I didn't know that!* This is usually spoken after you reveal some family secret you thought was common knowledge. Well, if your cousin replies *I didn't know that!* then you can be fairly certain it wasn't. You can also be fairly certain that it soon will be! It all depends on how you treat your cousin. And how your brother or sister treats them, because at the end of the day family loyalty can be bought and most cousins will sell to the highest bidder. So it might be worth keeping a stock of their favourite sweets handy, or being prepared to let them operate on your Sindy doll, even if it does make her eyes water (not to mention yours!).

Avoidance Tactics

If you live near your cousin it's quite likely that either your aunt or your mother will suggest joint family trips. Why they do this when they can't stand each other is one of life's great mysteries, but they still do it. In these instances it is rather hard to avoid your cousin. There are ways, obviously. For instance, if you're out on a family car trip you can wait till your mum's packing to go home and suggest a game of hide and seek. Assuming that you have the good sense to make sure your cousin shuts their eyes first, you should be able to get into the car and drive off before your hapless relative has counted to a thousand, unless the horrible little brat cheats. If luck is on your side you could drive hundreds of miles before they're missed. And if you want to go to the trouble of syphoning out some of the petrol you could ensure that there isn't enough to enable your mum to drive back and collect them.[1] Of course this may not be necessary, because mums can sometimes be relied on to refuse to drive back and collect cousins, depending on how much they like their own sister. Now all this may seem a bit extreme, but it depends on how much you want to avoid your cousin. You can of course just resort to the usual family tactics of bribery and threats.

1. With a bit more careful planning you could use this same method to get rid of your brothers and sisters at the same time, but you would have to wait till they'd all hidden. Do make sure that none of them are hiding under the car, won't you, because driving over a bump that wasn't there before can be a dead giveaway!

Daughter

Relationship

If you are the product of a moment of passion between your father and mother, you are probably their daughter, as long as you're female. If you are the product of a moment of anger and frustration between your father and an MFI flat-pack, you're probably a wobbly bookcase, as long as you're chipboard.

Habitat

It's usual for daughters to share a home with their parents, although they don't have to. Some may be away at boarding school, some may be living with other relatives for whatever reason, etc., etc. However, if you're a daughter and you're living in a cardboard box in the middle of your parents' lawn, this is very unusual.

Behaviour

If you're a daughter you will know that this can be very complex. As a general rule, although this is by no means a hard and fast one, daughters tend to be able to twist their dad around their little finger.[1] This obviously leads to trouble with brothers, not to mention mothers, so if you're a daughter, it's a tactic you should use very sparingly, in case your luck runs out!

1. The reverse tends to be true of sons. They tend to be Mum's favourite. But let a daughter get a boyfriend and watch Dad change!

Catch Phrase

Dad . . . usually said with wide eyes and an innocent look. This is quite difficult for some daughters to achieve, but can be done with practice. The result is usually worth the effort.

Avoidance Tactics...

It is actually impossible to avoid a daughter once they are determined not to be avoided. Believe me – I know!

FRONT VIEW

BACK VIEW

Elder....

In past times communities and families had elders. And of course in many communities (and most religions) this system still exists. Community Elders are usually elected leaders with religious or political status. Generally quite elderly, they are responsible for the spiritual and physical welfare of the community of which they are an elder. They can be found in a temple or community meeting place, and are there to help, counsel and advise. Their word is not law, but it is generally respected. Family elders are completely different.

Relationship

Family elders can be anything from a grandparent, uncle, elderly aunt, to a second cousin, etc. But before you get excited they are never a child! They are also never elected, except by themselves. In fact, in some cases they are the only person who is aware of the fact that they are an elder. They have no status other than the fact that they are old.

Habitat

They can be found in the most comfortable armchair, irrespective of whose house they're in, and they are there to annoy, interfere and decide what everyone is allowed to watch on TV.

Behaviour

Their word is not law, but if you dare to disagree with them, they will get their own back by muttering all the way through your favourite programme, leaving their teeth where you would least hope to find them, and generally causing as much trouble as possible.

Catch Phrase

You don't want to do that! would be their favourite expression. But if you find yourself tempted to say "If I didn't want to do it, I wouldn't do it," don't bother! This kind of basic logic is totally beyond their comprehension.

"You've Been Framed" is on the other side. This is another favourite phrase they use, usually to start a family feud. Why would they want to do that? I hear you ask. So that they can sort it out, of course, thus proving that despite the fact that they are eating you out of house and home and causing endless problems with the neighbours on account of their snoring and other little habits,[1] they are worth having around.[2]

Avoidance Tactics

Stay out of the house. Arrange for your meals to be passed through a window, or train the dog to carry them out to the garden shed.[3] Alternatively, arrange for a double-glazing salesman to pay the elder a personal call. There's nothing your average elder likes better than a nice long discussion about double glazing, alternative religions or anything where they can sound off. A word of warning: make sure they don't sign anything, or your parents may never forgive you, and you could all end up living in that cardboard box on the lawn!

1. Borrowing things is one of them. I'm sure nobody minds lending the odd cup of sugar or gardening implement, but we heard of one family elder who browbeat the next-door neighbours into lending her a complete fitted kitchen so that she could boil an egg! The poor neighbours were so intimidated they haven't had the guts to ask for it back!
2. They're not!
3. Or cardboard box in the middle of the lawn (*see also*: Daughter).

Father

I have actually covered fathers in more detail in my book *Coping With Parents*. However, a few additional hints might be helpful here.

Relationship

He's your father. What more can I say?

Habitat

Most of the time this species is to be found in an armchair behind a newspaper. This is always assuming that the family elder hasn't got there first, in which case he'll be hovering nearby, sighing a lot. On summer days he may be found standing around in the garden, desperately trying to look as though he knows what he's doing. After all, he's wearing a jumper just like the one the bloke on telly wears for gardening, knitted by an elderly aunt [*see also*: Aunt (Elderly)].

Behaviour

Girls, imagine the situation. You're standing on the front step of your home.[1] Your new boyfriend, Him from 5c, is currently whispering sweet nothings in your ear while he nibbles it. Sweet nothings like how much he loves you, how he can't live without you, how he'll die if you chuck him[2] ... OK, so he forgets your name a

---

1. Parents' house, not mental home! Although it's sometimes hard to tell the difference!
2. Before he has a chance to chuck you, anyway!

couple of times, but it's music to your ears. And then, over his shoulder, you notice the bushes move. This is very worrying. The bushes haven't so much as rustled slightly since your dad sprayed them with his home-made weedkiller. Someone's in the bushes! Who? A peeping Tom?[1] The guerrilla arm of the Local Authority, checking up on a late council tax return? Jeremy Beadle? No! The man in the Milletts army surplus flak jacket with Marmite smeared all over his face is your dad, checking up on you! Well, checking up on Him from 5c, actually.

And even though Dad hasn't done any exercise since he last turned the pages of his newspaper, just let Him from 5c get any funny ideas[2] and Action Man will be out of that bush with a bloodcurdling yell, asking Him from 5c how many GCSEs he's got and what his intentions are.[3] All because Dad loves you!

1. Why does Tom do all the peeping? What's wrong with Dick and Harry?
2. Funnier than whispering with a mouthful of ear, that is.
3. Judging from the shock that would give Him from 5c, I would imagine his intention would be to get out of there as fast as possible, and never come back!

Boys, you can't expect the same level of parental surveillance, I'm afraid.[1] Because a father's attitude towards his sons is totally different from his attitude towards his daughters. Whereas the majority of fathers make every effort to prevent any boy getting within four hundred miles of their beloved daughter, they positively encourage their sons to get as near everyone else's daughter as is humanly possible.[2]

Why is this? There seems to be a double standard at work here. Dad wants his son to be *a bit of a lad*, just like the *bit of a lad* he likes to think he was at that age.[3] The fact that no-one can ever remember him being *a bit of a lad* is neither here nor there. On the other hand, of course, they want their daughter to behave a lot better than some of the girls they met at that time. This isn't true of all dads, obviously. Some dads realise that if they taught their sons to respect other people's daughters, then other people's daughters would like them a whole lot more. But some dads never grow up. That's why some *other* dads have to hide in bushes!

Catch Phrase

When I was your age has been a popular favourite among dads for many generations. I think it's even part of the "Being a Man" pep talk that dads like to give their sons. In fact, in my case I think that's all my dad said to me. I was expecting to come away having learned the secrets of manhood: how to get a worm on a hook without getting worm blood all over Auntie Muriel's latest woollen masterpiece; how to answer the question "Are you 18?" without sounding as though you're lying,

1. As if you wanted it, eh guys?
2. And it's humanly possible to get pretty close, as you probably know!
3. It's a frightening thought, but everyone was young once, even dads!

even at 36 – stuff like that. Instead of which, my manhood training consisted of repeating *When I was your age* over and over until I could say it with the right degree of condescending sneer.

Get your hair cut was a very popular one with dads just after the last war. Now they tend to say: *Don't get your hair cut if it means having Bart Simpson shaved into it at the same time.*

D'you fancy a train set for Christmas? is Dad-speak for "I fancy a train set for Christmas, but I'm really too old to get away with buying one for myself, so I've got to pretend to be buying it for you, but just try and use it and you'll be for it!"

Avoidance Tactics...

Most dads regard their offspring with a sort of studied indifference. They like to think they should leave the day-to-day watering and pruning to Mum. But just try doing anything even vaguely interesting and watch your dad uncoil like a cobra. Like a cobra, but twice as deadly.

Other Advice

Take out a bit of insurance against the day that you really need Dad to agree to something. But there's no need to seek legal advice or enter into any expensive insurance policy. Just keep a photo of your dad handy – one taken when he thought of himself as *a bit of a lad*. I think you'll find it works every time!

Grandfather

Relationship

A grandfather is the father of either your mum or dad. In the case of your mum, he's called your *maternal grandfather*. In the case of your dad, he's called your *paternal grandfather*. In neither case will he necessarily show any maternal or paternal instincts.

Habitat

You can find grandfathers pretty well anywhere. For instance:

a) in a cosy little seaside cottage after a long and tiring bus journey;[1]

b) a few streets away in a house very similar to yours, except that his probably smells of mothballs;

c) in a small cupboard under your stairs.

In the case of c), it's as well to check that this particular grandfather is yours. Because although hiding in an under-stairs cupboard is a fairly odd thing to do, it's more common among grandfathers than you might imagine, and therefore the one in your cupboard could easily belong to someone else. If you recognise him, chances are he's yours, although it's just as likely that he could be wearing some form of fancy dress. Let's face it, anyone who hides in an under-stairs cupboard is capable of pretty well anything. If you're not sure whether he's yours or not, try and coax him out. Dog biscuits usually do the trick, I've found.

---

1. This is often the best type of grandfather! Near enough to visit, but far enough away to stop him causing trouble!

Behaviour

But why should a grown man behave in this peculiar fashion? Well, of course they don't all do it. Some of them behave very sensibly. Almost boringly, in fact. But your average grandfather can be relied upon to keep you entertained for hours, at no cost to yourself. But why do they do it? After all, weren't they once a father? You can't imagine a father behaving strangely, can you? He's far too busy hiding in bushes to protect his daughter, or playing with his son's train set. Well, yes. Grandfathers were once fathers, but they were also once children. And this is what influences them most in later life. It's known as "second childhood" and many grandfathers go through it, which can be good news for you, as it can provide you with an ally. It can also give you someone to play with. But a word of warning here: if you're going to let him join in your games, check what he got up to in the war first. If he tells you he used to be a dab hand at making explosives, either avoid him or take him on a trip to your school!

Catch Phrase

This really depends on what sort of a grandad he is. You see, there are so many different types. Some can be your best mate, while some turn out to be "elders" and say things like *You don't want to do that!*, in which case you'll be in for earache every time they come to visit. Some of them still remember being a dad and so they come out with things like *When I was your age.* The "second childhood" ones are more likely to say something like *I wonder what this does?* in which case you'd be wise to stick your fingers in your ears and run like the clappers!

Avoidance Tactics...

Again it depends on what type they are. In many cases, grandfathers provide many hours of (fairly) harmless fun, so there's no need to avoid them. If, however, they are elders or fathers in disguise, follow the advice previously given for these species. It may not work, though, because grandads can be a lot wilier than your average dad!

Other Advice

Never forget that although this person is your grandfather and you may be really happy about that, he's also your mother's (or father's) father and more than likely an uncle and a brother, too. This makes them very complex. Also remember that the further up the family tree you go, the thinner the branches get. This makes grandads very shaky and unpredictable. You have been warned!

Grandmother ....

Relationship

This species is the mother of either your mum or dad. In the case of your mum, she's called your *maternal grandmother*. In the case of your dad, she's called your *paternal grandmother*.

Habitat

A typical grandmother is like a mother hen, clucking over her brood. So you often find her at your elbow, whatever you're doing.[1] When they're not doing this, they're often found in their special chair.[2] Or in the kitchen, because grandmothers do like to cook. Or rather, they do like to feed people, which isn't always the same thing. There are many grandmothers who can't stand cooking, but still have a basic instinct to need to feed people. This must be very annoying for them. Just imagine it. You can't resist the urge to feed people, but you can't stand being in the kitchen. Who'd be a grandmother, eh? I wouldn't, but then I never will be.[3]

1. Even when you're in the loo. In fact this is one of their favourite places to surprise you!
2. They really do have a special chair. Unlike the elder, who just commandeers one and calls it their own, your average granny has worked hard to earn the family's respect and her own chair.
3. Not unless I offer up my body for some sort of genetic experimentation.

Behaviour

What is it about grandmas that makes them want to feed you up? I mean, you could be the size of a house, but your granny would still think you needed a nice big dinner inside you. Preferably something like cabbage, because that'll keep you regular. Because that's the other thing about grannies, isn't it? They do seem to be obsessed with keeping the family "regular". Why this should be I cannot even guess, but doubtless it's something that makes perfect sense when you're a granny. Just as elderly aunts are obsessed with knitting everyone a jumper, so grannies stuff everyone with food and natural laxatives.

Catch Phrase

Have you "been"? is obviously one of their favourites. They usually say this about ten minutes after they've said *Get that cabbage down yer. That'll keep you regular.* Maybe ten minutes is an exaggeration, because some grannies we've heard of have a special way of cooking cabbage that could get you going almost instantly!

Avoidance Tactics...

This is often very difficult because most grannies are sweet little old ladies who wouldn't harm a fly, and avoiding them would only offend them. (If you believe this then you're probably a bigger fool than you think you are!) Grannies are not easily offended. After all, they've had to put up with being related to your parents for all these years, so they must be very thick-skinned. If you're still worried about hurting Granny's feelings but you want to keep out of the way, can I suggest that you go under the stairs with Grandad – she won't even bother to look for you there!

Other Advice

Unless of course you actually *like* spending half your life chewing your way through Granny's homemade cabbage cake and the other half in the loo, you could try suggesting that she sends food parcels to Oxfam. That way she can channel her energies into doing some good. But try to discourage her from sending them her gravy.

G

Great-Aunt 🐧...

Relationship

Great-aunts are the sisters of either your grandfather or grandmother. This also makes them the aunts of either your mum or dad. It also makes them aunts-in-law, I suppose. Complicated, isn't it?

Habitat

This species tends to live a long way off. You may not even know that they exist, so check with your parents. Most people have got a great-aunt or two, but probably the only sign you ever get of their existence is a Christmas card that looks as if it's been written by a drunken spider. If you're really unlucky, you may get the occasional parcel of something that was probably meant to be a jumper for you. The fact that it doesn't fit and has got a couple of Care Bears on the front is normally due to the fact that she hasn't seen you since your christening and has forgotten how fast children grow. Still, with any luck you won't see her again for ages, so there's no danger of you suddenly having to cram yourself into the thing in case she gets offended.

Behaviour

It's not really that easy to offend this particular species. They tend to be very thick-skinned. Well, let's face it, they've had to suffer being related to your dad for years. Is this why they now live so far away? I think you should be told the truth. Oh yes, you were spun some story about Great-Aunt Mary running away to join the

60

circus, but having seen her photograph you had always assumed that this was only said to frighten you. You know the sort of things parents say: "Run away to join the circus and you could end up looking like your Great-Aunt Mary!" Not that you were ever taken in by this for a minute. After all, people who run circuses aren't stupid, are they? Let's face it, anyone who can train poodles to play better football than the England Squad has got to be fairly bright. So what possible reason would anyone that bright have for giving your Great-Aunt Mary a job?

No! I can't see that happening somehow! It's far more likely that Great-Aunt Mary moved so far away to put as much distance as possible between herself and a certain member of your family. Let's hope it wasn't you!

Catch Phrase

On the rare occasions that you see her (*see also* Births, Deaths, Marriages and Fights), your great-aunt tends to say things like *Who are you?* And if you bounce up to her with the enthusiasm of a great-niece or nephew who's pleased to see their great-aunt after such a long absence, beware. She's just as likely to think you're a mugger and yell out: *Come one step nearer and you'll be sorry! My son's a chartered accountant, you know!* Which of course is just the sort of thing that *would* frighten a would-be assailant. What does she imagine her son would do? Bore you to death with columns of figures? If you do let yourself get roped into going up and speaking to her (assuming she doesn't mistake you for a mugger), she'll probably express shock at your appearance and say something like *My, my! How you've grown!* What on earth does that mean? You've grown in exactly the same way as everyone else! Upwards mostly and a little bit sideways.

You were so small as a baby! That's another thing they say. Small as a baby? That's unusual, isn't it? I've never ever heard of that before, have you? But that's not all. Given half a chance, your great-aunt will regale you with tales of things you did as a child. Things that you obviously won't remember doing, because you were only a child. Things that, strangely enough, no-one else has ever mentioned you doing. Things that you eventually begin to realise you've probably never done. About now you realise that she's talking about someone else. You've been mistaken for your brother or sister – or both! This woman may not even be your great-aunt! She could be a total stranger who's wandered in off the street, eaten everything in the house and is now insisting on showing you photos of other total strangers!

Avoidance Tactics...

This can be quite easy, if you're subtle about it. The great-aunt isn't one for a lot of unnecessary movement. Why should she be? As long as there's someone topping up her teacup every few minutes,[1] she'll stay put.[2] So as long as you can avoid getting within eye-line or earshot, you should be OK. But before you relax, I ought to point out that this is not always as easy as it might seem. Great-aunts are like bats – they have extremely good hearing.[3] So either wear some thick padding on your feet,[4] or stay well away. Next door should be close enough. Of course if you do get spotted, then a quick exit is probably called for. If you have any influence with the Ministry of Defence, then you could probably arrange for the SAS to swoop in through the windows and snatch you from her clutches. But that might be going a bit over the top. Things like that tend to spoil normal family get-togethers. The only thing to do is arm yourself with a tray of sandwiches, so that you can use the excuse of handing them round to avoid having to chat with her for too long. There's only one problem with this otherwise brilliant plan – if you go within twenty feet of your great-aunt with a tray of sandwiches, she's likely to scoff the lot!

1. Where's she putting all this tea, and what's going to happen when it starts to spill out?
2. In the dog's favourite chair, probably. While the dog's still in it, probably. Not that the dog will complain. You won't hear him even if he does!
3. Some of them also hang upside down at night.
4. A couple of jumpers knitted by an elderly aunt should do the trick.

Husband

It's extremely unlikely (though not totally impossible) that you either are or have a husband. However, since you may well be or have one in the future, you may find this section useful. After all, you almost certainly *know* a husband – your dad's probably one!

Relationship

When a man is married to a woman, he is known as her husband. She is known as his wife. She may also be known as someone who ought to have had more sense than to get herself involved with him!

Habitat

A husband usually goes through various stages. A new husband will be found at his wife's side, dancing attendance, catering for her every whim, even laughing at her jokes (but only in very extreme cases). As the weeks go by, however, it becomes increasingly difficult to put your finger on him. Or even see him for that matter. There are a number of possible locations you might try: the garden shed,[1] the dog's basket[2] or behind that newspaper that appears to be levitating in front of the armchair.[3]

---

1. If there is one. If not, you may find him perched in the window box.
2. This is one of the reasons why he suggested getting a dog. The other one was so that he could take it for walks that involved going past a pub!
3. Let him enjoy it while he can. It won't be long before someone declares themselves a family elder and takes over this chair. The dog, probably!

Behaviour

Why should he keep disappearing like this? Well, it's all part of the way this particular species develops. You see, one day this husband will be a father, and therefore he has to prepare himself. The visits to the shed are to improve his woodwork skills. Chances are the most complicated thing this particular husband ever made at school in woodwork lessons was a door wedge.[1] Suddenly he's responsible for putting up shelves and so on. He will also probably want to try to give the impression that he knows something about gardening. Which of course he does – he knows the difference between a live and a dead flower. However, how to stop the former becoming the latter is still a complete mystery to him. The visits to the dog basket are to strike up a close relationship with the dog. Let's face it, once he has children the dog's probably going to be the only one who takes him seriously! And the armchair? Well, when all else fails, all he can do is try to pretend he isn't there!

Catch Phrase

Hi, honey! I'm home! This is what I think American TV would like to have you believe husbands say. And of course in the average American TV show, everyone – kids, wife, dogs, cats, goldfish – leap all over Dad and shower him with affection, just to show how pleased they are to see him, and how important they think he is. In real life things are very different. To begin with, he isn't the only one who's had a busy day. His wife may well have done a day's work, fitted in a bit of essential shopping in the lunch hour, rushed out of work to pick up the children, made them a meal while videoing Children's TV (so that they can watch it once she's done

---

1. Making a door wedge is not as easy as it sounds! I speak as one who knows!

their homework for them), got them bathed and into their pyjamas, and just had time to make a pot of tea before her husband gets home. You know, there must be some husbands who go to work early in the morning and get home late, and therefore probably think that their kids only wear proper clothes at the weekend. The rest of the time they wear pyjamas – even for school, probably! Of course some husbands know only too well what goes on while they're not there, and therefore know better than to make a big show of their homecoming. In fact, they positively creep in. Unfortunately, because they've spent many hours cultivating the affections of the dog, Fido only has to hear his master's key turning in the lock to start throwing himself around the room like a one-dog Highland Games. One tactic some husbands use in this situation is to launch into an explanation of why they're late home, whether they are or not. This is their way of saying: "I know you lot have had a busy day, but so have I." They start this the minute they step through the door (after sedating the dog). The explanation usually starts with *You wouldn't believe the traffic on the M25!*[1] and goes downhill from there. It isn't until they're ten minutes into the explanation and have got to the bit where they've been abducted by aliens but released after an hour of being forced to drink alien beer that the poor husband suddenly spots the note on the table: "Gone out with the girls. The freezer's full of food. Take your pick!"[2]

Avoidance Tactics.

Oh, please don't avoid him! He needs all the friends he can get! (*See also*: Wife.)

1. Even though they walk to work!
2. And if their freezer is anything like ours, he will have to take his pick! Ours hasn't been defrosted for years!

In-Laws

When a man and woman get married they do so because they want to spend the rest of their lives together,[1] just the two of them. Until they have a dog. Then children. Pets and children, generally speaking, are planned.[2] What neither party planned was getting an extra family. But they do, and that's often where the trouble starts!

Relationship

An in-law is anyone who is related by marriage. For instance: when a man marries a woman (and vice versa) the man's mother and father become his wife's mother- and father-in-law (and vice versa). Likewise the whole of the rest of the family become related in many and various ways.

Habitat

Since most in-laws have families of their own, the only time you're really likely to see them *en masse* as it were is at family events, so I've covered this species in more detail in the Births, Deaths, Marriages and Fights section of the book.

Behaviour

This varies incredibly, from the ridiculous to the even more ridiculous. I'm sure you already know this, having attended various family weddings, christenings etc., where the in-laws have been out in force. But before you start attacking your parents and asking them why on earth they wanted to get themselves involved with such a

1. Sadly it doesn't always work out that way, but that's the theory, anyway!
2. But even if they turn up unannounced they are generally wanted and loved.

bunch of maniacs,[1] I should point out that they weren't always like this. When your father started going out with your mum and she took him home for the first time, he probably met your mum's mum and dad.[2] If he was lucky, he might have met the odd[3] brother or sister.[4] The same thing would have happened when your father introduced his family to your mum for the first time. And, being on their best behaviour (and in love) they would have turned a blind eye to any suspicious scratching noises. How were they to know that these scratching noises were being made by the less socially acceptable members of the family, who had been locked in the under-stairs cupboard for the duration of the visit? It wasn't really until the wedding that either your mum or dad got to meet the other family in all their gory glory! Up until then Tracy and Linnette, the two monstrous bridesmaids who set fire to the vicar, were just names to your dad. Likewise your dad's cousin Shirley (who did your mum's hair for the Big Day and turned it green so that she had to get married with a Sainsbury's carrier bag on her head) was someone your mum had only ever heard of in the most glowing terms.

"You should let our Shirley do your hair for the wedding," your dad's family all said. "She could be a professional." Ah, yes! But a professional what? Certainly not a professional hairdresser!

Of course, all this happened long before you were born (probably!). But it does help to explain why some branches of your family don't talk to each other. They do shout at each other, but never talk!

1. Don't get too carried away. Remember that the in-laws are only the in-laws of one of your parents. They're the *family* of the other one!
2. Now your maternal grandparents.
3. Odd being the word!
4. Now your uncles and aunts.

Catch Phrase

In any conversation involving in-laws, you will hear phrases beginning; *Well, at least our (NAME)* . . . The next part of the sentence could be any one of the following:

. . . *has still got his own hair!*

. . . *isn't a convicted criminal!*

. . . *has never been photographed wearing a dress!*

etc., etc. No, it doesn't take in-laws long to start slinging the mud – sometimes literally!

Avoidance Tactics...

It's really *you* I feel sorry for, because you've got two lots of in-laws! You've got your mum's in-laws and your dad's. And, although you know them as grannies, grandpas, aunts, uncles, cousins, etc., when the chips are down they revert to being in-laws.[1] The best advice I can offer is, next time you're at a family gathering, quickly organise a game of *Wake up the sleepy old relative and watch them jump!*, which should keep you out of harm's way. But remember to involve your cousins. After all, they're suffering from the in-laws just as much as you are!

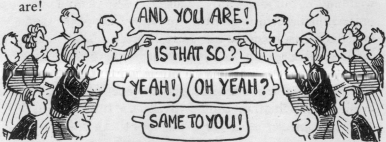

1. Like the time the chips were down the front of Auntie Mary's dress! What a family feud that started! I suppose it wouldn't have been so bad if Great Uncle Eric hadn't started trying to retrieve them! He didn't stop until your second cousin Dave threw a bucket of water over him. Then Uncle Simon's pitbull joined in . . .

Junior

This is really an Americanism, although it's becoming more popular over here.

SENIOR   JUNIOR

Relationship

"Junior" is the term used to describe a first-born son, who has been given the same first name as his father, for some strange reason. As if it isn't hard enough surviving family life without that to contend with! This is very much a male thing. There may be instances of girls being named after their mother, and called "Junior", but I haven't come across any. Personally, I think mums have got more sense! Naturally there are millions of cases of girls being named after their fathers, by which I don't mean they get called Derek, but rather they get given a female version of their dad's name. Thus:

William becomes Wilhelmina; Eric becomes Erika; John becomes Joan; Peter becomes Petra, etc., etc. You get the idea! This may well have happened to you. You have my sympathy!

Habitat

As close to Dad as possible. Sometimes this is from choice, sometimes not. Quite often the father doesn't stop at calling his son after himself – he gives him scaled-down versions of his belongings (same jumper,[1] same silly trousers, same tool-kit so that he can help daddy make the shelves fall down . . .)

Behaviour

Initially Junior behaves exactly like his older namesake. This is because he's encouraged to do so. After a very short time though, being Junior (or "Little Man" or any of the other diminutives that go with this particular situation) becomes rather embarrassing[2] and he starts to try to avoid family gatherings where this situation can be exploited. Not least because Junior's brothers and sisters tend to resent the favouritism that being named after one's father suggests. But it's not Junior's fault. He didn't pick his name or choose to be a miniature clone of his dad,[3] did he? But what can he do? Hide under the stairs? What, and have grandad blurt out "What are you doing in here, Junior?" No! All he can do is grin and

---

1. Knitted, incidentally, by the same elderly aunt.
2. Certainly by the time you're thirty it's lost most of its novelty value!
3. Let's face it, you'd have to be seriously warped to want to be a clone of your dad!

bear it, and hope that one day his dad will realise that he's a person in his own right and stop treating him like a reflection.

Catch Phrase

Dad . . . This is said in a pleading, long-suffering fashion. Basically it's short for *Dad, please don't say such inane things because everybody thinks that I think like you do, and I don't want them to think I'm a prat as well.* Obviously it's quicker just to say *Dad . . .*

Avoidance Tactics...

You shouldn't really avoid a Junior. He's got enough to put up with, just being lumbered with the tag. Likewise if *you're* a Junior there's not much you can do. Eventually relatives will stop referring to you as Junior and start calling you by your proper name. Of course, then they have the problem of what to call your dad! But don't worry, I'm sure they'll think of something!

Other Advice

This is more for the chaps than the girls. When the time comes for you to get married and "increase your tribe", you may find yourself thinking: "Wouldn't it be a great idea to name my son after myself and call him Junior!" No. It really wouldn't! Trust me!

Kin...

Not a term that you hear every day, but one occasionally used.

Relationship

The term kin refers to anyone who is related by blood – mother, father, sister, brother, grandparents, etc. Your *next of kin* is the person who stands to inherit your estate in the event of your death. Not that you need to worry about that yet, but that's what it means, OK?

Habitat

Scattered all over the place. In fact, we've probably all got kin that we don't even know about. At least we have if *Surprise Surprise* is anything to go by!

Behaviour

Just because they're kin, and this makes them sound a bit more important and up-market, don't be fooled. They're still relatives and behave just as appallingly!

Catch Phrase

See every other entry!

Avoidance Tactics...

Likewise, see every other entry!

Other Advice

If you have to fill out a form that asks you to name your next of kin, make somebody up. It'll serve them all right, particularly if you've got anything worth inheriting!

which brings us very neatly to . . .

Long-Lost Relative ...

You must have seen articles in newspapers under headlines such as *I AM PHIL FINKLY'S[1] FORGOTTEN UNCLE*. There then follows a long, heart-jerking article explaining how, although this particular relative has never met his famous nephew and has never in fact lived on the same planet, he is single-handedly responsible for his nephew's fame. And (wouldn't you know it?) his nephew has never so much as given him a cup of tea! Not that he wants anything, you understand. He just happens to find himself chatting to a journalist who just happens to say "Has anyone ever told you you look like Phil Finkly's long-lost uncle, the one that no-one's ever heard of?" Suddenly a long-lost relative is born. Although they're not in it for the money, you understand . . .

Relationship

Who knows? They're usually a relative that no-one can actually remember, even though one of your aunties is supposed to have been married to this character for fifty years! Well, if she can't remember him, what chance have the rest of us got?

Habitat

Well, according to him, he's been living in a cardboard box. But before you can say, "Oh, yes! I know those cardboard boxes! They're not bad!" he adds: "in Africa", where he's been working as a missionary, naturally!

1. You must have heard of Phil Finkly! He's the really, really famous superstar who starred in that film about . . . no! Hang on! He had a record at number one for . . . or is he that brain surgeon? Anyway, he's really famous!

Behaviour

Ah! This is what it's all about! As soon as he's eaten everything in the fridge, behaving exactly like somebody who hasn't eaten for about four years,[1] he explains how he was more than happy working away selflessly for the poor and needy in Africa and he only looked you up because he was worried about you. It's got absolutely nothing to do with your recent bit of good luck.[2] He just thought he'd look you up. However, if you're worried about how to spend your new fortune, he does have a foolproof[3] investment plan he could push your way.[4] If you're wise you hang on to your cash. After all, it's not every day you win five pounds in a crossword competition. Watch his face when you tell your long-lost relative that that's the extent of your windfall!

Catch Phrase

I'll look after your wallet for you if you like. He fails to add: *In case some unscrupulous person tries to steal it!* in case you think he's talking about himself!

Avoidance Tactics ...

This is difficult because the average long-lost relative is very believable. After all, he's probably had a lot of practice being other people's long-lost relatives!

1. This, he explains, is nothing to do with hunger. He's suffering from a rare form of Mad Cow Disease. He caught it when he was married to your aunt, he adds with a chuckle.
2. This good luck could be anything from a win on a Premium Bond to the fact that you've invented a non-meat spam sandwich, and Linda McCartney has invited you to go into business with her.
3. Foolproof, of course, until you happen to be fool enough to get involved!
4. Amazingly, when this sort of thing happens in real life and not just in a silly book, no-one ever says: "Oh, yeah? If you've got this foolproof investment plan, how come you're living in a cardboard box?"

Mother...

Relationship

Your mother is the woman who gave birth to you. Everyone has a mother or used to have one. If you honestly believe you've never had a mother in your life, then check your drawers. If you've got three you're probably a sideboard.

Habitat

In Victorian times (when Great-Granny was a little girl) it was quite easy to find this particular species of family member. They were in the kitchen, cooking or washing. This was pretty well a full-time job because, no matter how hard Victorian kids tried, they still got dirty and hungry. These days things are a bit different. Many mothers work.[1] Children, however, still get dirty and need feeding. So Mum usually ends up doing that as well. Oh, of course, some dads help – mainly with the fun things like cooking or taking the kids out to play football, etc. Rarely, if ever, do they help with the really boring things like washing-up and hoovering. Can you blame them? I mean, do *you* like washing-up? Honestly? Neither do I! But it still has to get done. And if nobody else rolls their sleeves up, Mum usually takes it on. Incidentally, when dads do it, they tend to want a medal at least. They'll come into the room, dripping washing-up water all over the cat, and say "I'm doing the washing up!" This is your cue to take a photo or phone the local

---

1. Hence the expression *working mum*. This expression is used to distinguish between working mums and mums who only work when you plug them in.

paper, because if you don't record this moment for posterity he'll sulk for ever, so be warned! Mum wants no such accolades. She just wants to turn the pile of dirty dishes into a pile of clean ones, without turning the whole operation into *The Paul Daniels Show*.[1]

Behaviour

Not only is Mum the Head Cook and Bottlewasher, she's also the Law! Oh, yes! There's no doubt about that! OK, so your dad might be the one who does the telling off, but he's only following orders. If you don't believe me, then next time Dad gives you an ear-bashing say to him, "Why are you giving me such a hard time, Dad?" I bet you any money you like that your dad will reply: "Keep your voice down! Your mum'll hear you!" Try it! See if I'm right! But why should this be? Well, it's

1. You'll soon realise that this is one of the big differences between mums and dads.

another of those unpleasant tasks that have to be done
but don't win any prizes. In fact, making sure everyone
keeps the house rules can make a person unpopular, and
dads don't like being unpopular. Mums don't either,
but more importantly they want a hassle-free home. Oh,
yes! Make no mistake about it, in the average household,
Mum is Queen Bee and Dad's just a drone.

Catch Phrase

Wait till your dad gets home. This basically means that
Mum's telling you off, but wants Dad to share the
blame. So: Dad will come home, Mum will tell him to
tell you off and he will then tell you off, even though he

hasn't got the foggiest idea what he's telling you off for, and even though you already feel thoroughly told off by Mum. So go along with it – it's all part of the game.

Ask your father. This means "no", but is another example of Mum trying to split the blame for doing something unpopular with Dad. This isn't unique to mums, though. Dads do it just as much. More, in fact.

I'll slap you in a minute! This is usually said just *after* she's slapped you, for some strange reason. Of course, these days fewer and fewer parents slap their children, mainly because it hurts. I mean a slap on the back of the leg can give you a sore hand for hours!

Tidy your room! This is only ever said because Mum feels that the house is too quiet. It has absolutely nothing to do with wanting you to tidy your room. No mother seriously imagines that you will, anyway![1]

I'm not coming in your room until you've tidied it. This is the sort of thing mums say without thinking. If they stopped to think they'd realise that, far from being a threat, it's a promise!

Avoidance Tactics...

Avoiding Mum is almost impossible. They're as nimble as ninjas and can sneak around the house without a sound.[2] The way to avoid her is to wait till she's just said *I'm not coming in your room until you've tidied it*, and then stay in your room. If you intend to do this for any length of time, though, make sure you take a telephone in with you, plus the number of a good take-away and Dad's credit card!

---

1. "Tidy" means different things to different people, anyway. As far as you're concerned, having everything exactly where you want it, so that you can lay your hands on it quickly may be the perfect state to be in.
2. Unlike Dad who comes in late, takes his shoes off so that he doesn't make a noise, then trips over the cat!

New Arrival

Yes! It's time to talk babies!

Relationship

This depends on a number of things. If it's dressed in pink, it's probably a sister. If it's dressed in blue, it's probably a brother. If it's got its giblets in a plastic bag, it's probably an oven-ready turkey. Why do they do that?[1] In this day and age, when pretty well anything goes fashion-wise, why do many (if not most) parents insist on dressing their newborn baby in pink (for girls) or blue (for boys)? Well, actually there are a number of reasons. The two most obvious, and practical, are:

1) To help the doctors tell the difference. Let's face it, if you were a hospital doctor and hadn't slept for seventy-two hours, you might need a bit of help.

2) To help passers-by, and the mother. Imagine you're a mum. OK, for some of you boys that might be tricky, but try. You've not long left hospital, you're still feeling a bit shaky, and you're venturing out for the first time pushing your brand-new pram, which contains your brand-new baby. New prams are like a magnet. Total strangers and people who positively *hate* kids will stop a mother pushing a pram, so that they can jam their head into the hood and coo over the baby. This continual stopping is very tiring for the mother, as you can probably imagine (even you boys!). Particularly when she has to answer the same questions every time:

---

1. I'm not referring to oven-ready turkeys. The fact that they have their giblets in a bag is just one of those quirks of nature.

PASSER-BY: What a lovely baby! What is it?
NEW MUM: A girl.
PASSER-BY: What do you call her?
NEW MUM: Marianne.
PASSER-BY: What a lovely name! (*pause*)
Erm . . .
(*Passer-by wanders off.*)

Now this may not seem much to you, but multiply it by a hundred, add to that the fact that the poor new mum has been up six times during the night to feed the baby, wind it, change it, cuddle it, etc., and you can probably see that their brief walk could turn into a nightmare. However, if the baby's dressed in the colour associated with its sex, the conversation is cut in half, thus:

PASSER-BY: What a lovely baby girl! What do you call her?
NEW MUM: Dave.
PASSER-BY: Oh! (*pause*)
Erm . . .
(*Passer-by wanders off*)

Not much of a saving, you might think, but multiply by a hundred, etc., and it soon mounts up!

Habitat

Often found heavily wrapped in blankets, new arrivals are often mistaken for bundles of washing. This species is also found in bed with your mum and dad when you're not allowed in there, and in the sink when you want to give your pet frog diving lessons.

WHERE DID I PUT THAT BABY?

Behaviour

Being very small, new arrivals don't do much, although they make a great deal of noise not doing much. They still have quite an impact on the behaviour of the rest of the family, however. If you're quite young when the new arrival is imminent, your mum and dad make a big fuss of you. This is in case you're jealous. They offer to buy you a new toy, so that you've got something new as well as them. They're not very happy when you say: "Can I have a new toy *instead* of a new baby?", which seems unfair because a Sega Megadrive is a lot less bovver than a bruvver! When the baby actually arrives your parents encourage you to hold it and cuddle it. This is strange, because they then spend the next ten years dragging you apart.[1] Naturally, you're not keen to hold the baby, in case it's sick all over you – or worse. Because, let's face it, there's not much else for a baby to do, really. And realising that that gawky-looking geezer is its dad is enough to make anybody throw up!

Catch Phrase

Goo goo gar gar! This is usually said over and over, although nobody takes much notice. They should, because it actually means: "Watch out, because one day I'll be a younger brother!"[2]

---

1. This is supposedly in case you kill each other!
2. Or sister which, as we all know, is much, much worse!

Avoidance Tactics...

This is difficult, when your parents are going out of their way to make you and your little brother/sister love each other. One way to be pretty sure of not being asked to cuddle or look after the baby too much is to develop a twitch. Something that happens at the mention of babies. Something that might suggest that you're allergic to them, perhaps. Just a gentle but unpredictable twitch will do. Don't go over the top – there are no Oscars for this performance. Oh, and make sure the twitch happens *before* the baby's placed in your arms! Babies don't bounce, even the hideously fat ones!

Old Man

Supposedly a term of affection for your father. Be careful how you use it, though. He might be feeling his age! (*See also*: Father.)

O

Older Brother 🚶📖....

Relationship

Your older brother is anyone who is male, older than you, and has the same father and mother. Don't confuse them with half-brothers. A half-brother is anyone, of whatever age, who has either the same father or the same mother as you, but not both, or is totally invisible from the waist downwards.

Habitat

They are generally found in the same house as you. They're also found in the bathroom just when you want to go in there. They have a nasty habit of turning up behind doors, sofas or even cupboards just when you're doing something that could get you into trouble.[1]

Behaviour

Extremely odd usually, particularly if they've got a girlfriend. On these occasions they stop smelling like the bottom of the ornamental fishpond after the dog has drunk all the water,[2] and start smelling like a cross between a field of dead flowers and a bottle of disinfectant.[3] Just why do they spend so much time in the bathroom? OK, so they don't disappear in there with a

1. To be fair to you, this is usually something totally innocent, but by the time your brother has embellished it a bit and told your mum, the original "crime" has become a hanging offence!
2. And been rushed to the vet's.
3. Which is a pity because, according to the advert, they should smell like a surf-wave crashing on a sun-drenched beach.

picnic hamper for days on end like older sisters do (*see also*: Older Sister), but they do take an age. Some older brothers spend so long in the bathroom that you'd have time to grow a beard while you were waiting for them to come out. So what are they doing in there? Not admiring themselves in the mirror, that's for sure! They must have given that up as a waste of time years ago. More than likely they're checking for hairs on their chin. You see, older brothers are desperate to be able to grow a beard, even though most girls don't like them, most schools don't allow them, and most parents will make them shave it off! Ah, puberty! That time of your life when your chin becomes a battlefield on which the spots and the hairs fight to outnumber each other. Some older brothers try squeezing away the spots to make more room for the hairs.[1] After all, they've been behind the bike sheds and they know a thing or two about human biology. Unfortunately, they don't know enough to realise that an inflamed hair follicle can look like a spot, especially if you're looking at it with nothing between your face and the mirror apart from a huge magnifying glass. Poor big bruv! He must squeeze away more beards than he could get on a multitude of chins! But try telling him, and see where it gets you! Nowhere! Why? Because big brothers know everything. They may only be a year older than you, but to hear them talk you'd

1. Hardly any brothers at all pick out the hairs to make more room for spots!

think they'd sailed forty times round the world with the navy! A man of the world at fourteen! Can you believe it? About the only thing they actually know that you don't is how to start trouble and convince your parents it was your fault without even speaking!

Catch Phrase

They have several of these. The most pathetic one is *And you are*! Why do kids say that to each other? OK, so sometimes it's true.

"You're human!"
"And you are!"

But other times it's blatantly untrue and shows that the person saying it is totally lacking in imagination. So the next time anyone insults you, particularly your younger brother/sister, don't say "And you are!" – use your imagination. You spend hours at school every day, broadening your knowledge and improving your

vocabulary, so use it to floor your sibling. Say something like . . . er . . . erm . . . Oh, OK, stick with "And you are"!

You'll understand when you're older. This is something older brothers[1] are very fond of saying. This is all part of their thing about being much more worldly wise than you are, even though they go to the same school, have the same teachers and everything. What are they being taught that you're not? Older brothers often use this particular catch-phrase when they think they're in love. Love!?! You've seen this girl before. In fact, didn't your brother use to frighten her with frogs? And now here he is dribbling all over her school jumper. Let's face it, the only reason you can think of for kissing a girl is to try and nick her chewing gum. But when you point this out to your brother, what does he say? Yes! *You'll understand when you're older.* The sad thing is, it usually turns out that he's right!

Avoidance Tactics...

Older brothers are quite difficult to avoid. Like bad pennies and non-specific rashes, they have a nasty habit of turning up when you least expect or want them. However, if they walk in on you and your mates unannounced, you can get rid of them pretty quickly by saying "Oh, I'm glad you've turned up. We were just about to look at these old photos." Works every time!

1. And older sisters for that matter.

Older Sister

Relationship

Obviously she's your sister, daughter to your mum and dad, and she's older than you!

Habitat

More so than an older brother, this species can be found in the bathroom. In fact, if you've got an older sister I would suggest that you spend your pocket money on shares in your local water company.

Behaviour

But why does she spend so much time in the bathroom? Well, it's so that she can make herself look prettier.[1] Now you may think that the only way she's going to do that is to have a complete head transplant, but then you've seen her first thing in the morning and nobody's at their best first thing in the morning.[2] Even the school gerbils look pretty jaded before lunch. Mind you, that's hardly surprising, the things they have to endure in the name of medical science! Anyway, somebody must think your big sister's pretty. Your dad's always saying how attractive she is. But then he married your mum, didn't he? So maybe he's a bad example! Still, she always seems to have plenty of boyfriends. She can't be bribing them all to go out with her. After all, she's very short of cash once she's paid you protection money.

1. Or just pretty!
2. Even *Take That* must look pretty awful first thing in the morning.

The other thing about big sisters is the fact that they like ordering you around, don't they? When they're not in the bathroom, that is. And even when they are they shout through the keyhole. And the older they get, the more they start to sound like your mum. Perhaps they're practising for when they'll be Boss in their own house. What an awful thought! Not only is some poor sucker going to make the mistake of marrying your big sister,[1] but she's probably going to have children of her own. So before you start feeling sorry for yourself for being her younger brother/sister, spare a thought for the poor unfortunates who will one day be calling her "Mum"!

Catch Phrase

Are you completely stupid? This is a popular one with older sisters. In fact they're very keen on anything that sounds vaguely like a put-down. As it happens, you must be a bit stupid because you're related to her and she's a total idiot!

1. If they can get her out of the bathroom long enough!

Avoidance Tactics...

Stay away from the bathroom. That way you'll probably only have to put up with her at mealtimes, and even she is too well brought-up to talk with her mouth full. Many of you may have already realised that avoiding the bathroom isn't that much of a hardship. After all, what's the point of washing? You only get dirty again! And teeth only fall out when you clean them!

Other Advice

I suppose I should point out that although you may feel hard done by having to put up with a big sister, she's having to put up with a younger brother or sister (you!). Although that's her fault for being older than you, isn't it?

Parent

A collective term for your father and mother. (*See* Father/Mother.)

Pets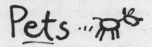

Yes, pets are family too!

Relationship

Unless you have webbed feet and feathers all over your bottom, that duck on your lawn is just a pet, not a blood relative.

Habitat

Pets are found where and when they want to be. They will ignore all attempts to make them conform. If you don't believe me, just try sticking their name on the washing-up rota and see if it gets done!

Behaviour

Not being an actual blood relative won't stop your average pet insisting on taking its full and equal place as a member of the family. They'll expect to be a party to any family decisions that may be made, even though most of them can't speak our language. They'll expect to be allotted their own special chair. They'll also expect to be allowed to change their special chair for your special chair at a moment's notice. Don't try to fight this. Just go with the flow, because anything you try to do will not work. One of my research team met a family who had a scaled-down replica of their home in the back garden, complete with all mod-cons and a leatherette three-piece suite, just for their pet toy poodle. However, Arnold (the poodle) wasn't having any of it. He still came ambling into the room every evening to play his version of non-musical chairs. Even when the family all moved into the scaled-down home it made no difference – Arnold just moved in with them! So be warned. A pet can be the most troublesome member of your family!

Catch Phrase

Woof! In the case of a dog, anyway. The odd rabbit[1] has been known to go *Woof!* but it's not common.[2] But, whatever particular catch phrase your pet favours, whether it be a woof, squeak or roar, it all boils down to the same thing in the end. They're just reminding you who's in charge! (*See also*: Elder.)

1. Very odd rabbit, obviously.
2. Unlike rabbits, who are very common. They also have appalling table manners.

MATCH THE SOUND TO THE PET COMPETITION

A	WOOF
B	WOOF
C	WOOF
D	RARROOOOOOO
E	FRITT-FRITT
F	SSP
G	VEEEP VEEEEP
H	PRAKA PRAKA PRAKA

Avoidance Tactics...

Just another family member who's difficult to get away from, however hard you try. They always seem to know if you don't like them, and react accordingly. This usually takes the form of sitting on you and licking you all over.[1]

Other Advice

Of course, you don't have to have a pet. They're not compulsory. Getting one isn't something that should be entered into lightly, however cute and fluffy they may look in the shop window.[2] A dog in particular needs a lot of exercise – it isn't enough just to buy it a multi-gym. Remember, a dog is for life,[3] not just for Christmas.[4]

---

1. Pet lions are especially fond of doing this!
2. Often the dog you see in the window isn't actually the one you wind up with. This is because many pet shops employ specially trained animal models, who have attended animal drama school and taken cuteness lessons. The mutt you end up with is a lookalike who can't even spell 'cute' let alone be it!
3. When I say *life*, it's actually a bit like a prison sentence. Life means 15-20 years. Possibly less with good behaviour.
4. Personally, I always have a turkey.

Quads 𝍤𝍤𝍤𝍤

Occasionally a mother will give birth to four children at the same time. Well, one after the other, anyway! Sometimes this is because there is a history of quads in the family. If you're not sure whether this applies to your family, think about your relatives. Do you, for instance, have a cousin who always seems to be in four places simultaneously, and can change sex at will? If so, he/she is probably quads. If he/she isn't, you should contact the *Guinness Book of Records* immediately. (*See also*: Sextuplets.)

Relationship

Quads could be your brothers and sisters, uncles and aunts, or cousins. You could be a quad yourself. It's unlikely that quads could be your mother or father, although one of them might be.

Habitat

Quads will be found wherever there's four of anything: four high-chairs, four cots, four piles of smelly nappies, etc.

Behaviour

Because quads are born at the same birth, it's often assumed that they'll think and react alike. Certainly, as with twins, there are cases of quads being almost telepathic, but it's not always the case. Not that it makes a lot of difference to you if you're on the receiving end. Four people with one opinion ganging up on you is only marginally worse than four people with different opinions ganging up on you. But obviously it's much worse for their poor parents, especially when they're very young. Imagine trying to feed four toddlers at the same time, and trying to remember which one hates peas, which one likes their egg runny on the top, and which one will only eat dog biscuits. It's hard enough coping with one small child, but four!

Catch Phrase

And me. This is a popular catch phrase with quads. It's usually said after one of its brothers/sisters has said *Can I have a drink, Mum.*[1] But it's never said while Mum's pouring a drink for quad number 1, oh, no! Quad number 2 waits till Mum has put the squash bottle back in the cupboard, and gone back to her seat in front of the telly to watch her favourite Aussie soap. Just as she's settling on the chair, Quad 2 pipes up. Naturally, Quad 3 does the same thing a few minutes later. Quad 4 follows on eventually, just so that he/she doesn't get left out.

---

1. They know better than to ask Dad. He'll make such a performance out of it, and expect so much praise for doing it, that they'll have gone off the idea by the time they get it!

Avoidance Tactics...

Of course, Mum will try to avoid this sort of thing by asking, as she pours the first drink, "Do any of you others want one?" The three remaining quads will naturally say: "No, thanks." Until Mum starts to sit down. Now, you may say, "So what? Mums get used to that sort of thing!" Yes, fair enough! But just think – if they can cause that kind of strife for their mum, what could they do to you, as their brother or sister?

Other Advice

Stay away from them. (*See also*: Sextuplets.)

Quite Nice Relative ...

There's no such thing!

Relations :

This is the collective term for all family members, whether blood relatives or related by marriage. There are other collective terms for specific groups of relatives. For instance:

A pat of younger brothers – because they're always covered in mud.

A sneer of older brothers – because that's what they always seem to do.

A cloud of older sisters – watch her as she comes out of the bathroom, on her way to a big date. You'll see exactly what I mean. You'll also see exactly what happened to that expensive talcum powder you saved so hard to buy your mum for Christmas!

A sigh of mothers – especially when she also sees what happened to that very expensive talc, etc., etc!

A grunt of fathers – especially when Mum tells him to have a word with big sister about using the expensive talc, etc., etc.

A *fun-pack of uncles* – because they always seem to have more fun with their kids (your cousins) than you and your family have. Don't be fooled. This is just for show. At home they're exactly the same as your dad.

A *clique of cousins* – because they always seem to be plotting some terrible prank. (*See* Births, Deaths, Marriages and Fights.)

A *click of elderly aunts* – because they always seem to be knitting some terrible pullover.

A *scrabble of grannies* – but only if you're prepared to let them cheat, make up words, and eventually win!

A *scrabble of grandpas* – but only if they're locked under the stairs again (usually for challenging Granny's Scrabble score)!

Sister

Pretty well everyone has a sister, or *is* a sister. They can be found in your wardrobe, in your record collection, in your clothes when you're not wearing them – in fact almost anywhere that you don't want them to be. And like brothers, they come in two varieties: younger and older. If you want to know how to cope with them, check the relevant entry.

Sextuplets

The usual way that a mother gives birth to sextuplets is after taking a special fertility drug. Ironically, this is usually because she's desperate to have a baby. Notice I said *a* baby, meaning one. So she takes this special drug and ends up with *six*, thus proving the old saying: "It never rains but it pours!"[1]

1. Whatever that means!

Relationship

Sextuplets are the sons and daughters of a man and a woman.[1] They could be your brothers, sisters or cousins, or you could be one of the six yourself.

Habitat

This species is often found in a row. This is because feeding six children at the same time is easier if it's done on a conveyor belt! Just imagine! Six! It must come as a terrible shock! The big problem with having six children at once is the fact that the average parents only have one pair of hands each. So cuddling six crying babies simultaneously becomes impossible. Usually any parents with sextuplets have to get relatives, baby-sitters or even nannies to help. This obviously becomes expensive, which is why parents of sextuplets have to try to get sponsorship. By this I mean that they get given free nappies, say, in return for advertising them. Of course it may not always be possible to get the same firm to sponsor all six babies, and this can lead to problems. Imagine if each child was sponsored by a different nappy firm, and they all had to wear a T-shirt advertising their particular product. Obviously they wouldn't be allowed to go out together, because the different advertising slogans would cancel each other out. But if they didn't all go out together, no-one would realise that they *were* sextuplets, and the advertising would be wasted! It's obviously not easy having sextuplets!

1. And sometimes a test-tube!

Behaviour

I remember when the Walton sextuplets were born a few years ago, their parents said they had very different personalities almost from birth. So presumably their behaviour would be like quads, only half as bad again! (*See also*: Quads.)

Catch Phrase

Ask my brother/sister. That's about the worst thing a sextuplet could say, because where would it end? You could be going around in circles for days without getting an answer. Mind you, maybe that's why they say it in the first place!

Avoidance Tactics...

A bit difficult to avoid, because they always come mob-handed. If you're related to them, you just have to hope they're not older than you, otherwise you'll never get in the bathroom!

Twins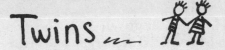

By comparison with sextuplets or quads, twins should be easy to handle. But only by comparison!

Relationship

Twins are two children (boys, girls or a combination) who are born within minutes of each other to the same mother. Therefore two babies born on the same day in the same hospital are not necessarily twins. Especially if they're born in different rooms.

Habitat

Look for a twin, and you'll usually find two. Because that's the kind of species this is – a stick-together species.

Behaviour

Identical twins often enjoy pretending to be each other. Some even claim that their own parents can't tell them apart. Well, to quote an old expression, I blame the parents. After all, if you're having trouble telling one twin from the other, why dress them in identical outfits, even if you do think it looks cute?[1] Why not label them? After all, salt and pepper pots are the same, but you never get those muddled up, do you? Mind you, this is probably due to the number of holes in the top of each pot. I don't think the same method would work for twins, somehow. But it does seem to be a fact that some twins get enormous pleasure out of confusing everyone

1. It doesn't!

by switching places. However, in private twins behave exactly like real people! It's true! They argue and fight just like normal brothers and sisters. I know this to be true because I once disguised myself as one of a pair of identical twins, and spent an entire afternoon in intimate chit-chat with my supposed sister. She didn't suss me at all. It just goes to show how close some twins actually are, doesn't it? Anyway, we had a real blazing argument about who's turn it was to use the hairdryer. It was stupid really because I was wearing a cheap acrylic wig.[1] Anyway, it soon became quite obvious to me that, apart from having a clone, twins are quite ordinary.

Catch Phrase

Ask my twin. That's a popular one with twins. It's all part of the "I bet you can't tell us apart" gag.

Avoidance Tactics...

Twins are a bit like buses. You don't see one for ages, then two come along together. They're quite hard to avoid, though. However, if you want to get them to leave you alone, just keep mixing them up after they've stopped playing their little twins game and told you which is which. It really gets them going! (Always assuming that you can be bothered to get them going!)

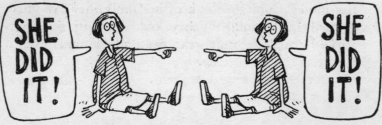

1. Which actually looked better than the real thing!

Uncle .....

Relationship

Any male who is the brother of your mother or father, or is married to the sister of your father or mother, is your uncle. I say male rather than man, because it's perfectly possible for you to have an uncle who is younger than you. Say, for instance, that your grand-parents have your mother at a young age, then have another child late in life, and in the meantime your mum has married your dad and had you, then your mum's younger brother would be your uncle. Confused? I'm not surprised!

Habitat

Uncles can be found anywhere – anywhere that's *fun*, that is, because uncles like having fun. That's always been my impression, anyway. You know the situation: you visit your cousins for the day and your uncle, their dad, is the life and soul of the party. You find yourself looking at your own dad and thinking: "Why can't he be like that?" Of course I realise now that I only ever saw my uncles at Christmas, birthdays, weddings and other jolly occasions, so I probably never saw them in every-day mode. Come to think of it, I only ever saw them dressed up. Presumably they looked scruffy occasion-ally. I mean, you can't wear a suit all the time, even if you're the Prime Minister.[1]

1. Actually, I'm not sure that's true. I have been told that the present Prime Minister sleeps in a suit.

Behaviour

An uncle's behaviour seems to depend on what grade of relative they are. By that I mean whether they're a brother of your father/mother, or an uncle by marriage. Uncles by marriage tend to behave themselves slightly better, I suppose because they aren't quite "family". In these cases, their wife (your auntie) usually makes up for this by causing enough family trouble for both of them!

A blood-related uncle's behaviour, on the other hand, is determined by whether they are the older or younger brother of your mum/dad. Younger brother uncles (if you can follow that!) can be more fun, because they've usually got more things to get back at their older brother/sister for. So beware this type of uncle, because he may use you to get at your mum or dad. And they can get devious. Beware, for instance, the uncle who insists on paying for you to go on all the really fast bumpy rides when you go to the fair, then keeps buying you candy-floss and ice cream. He's just trying to get you to throw up in your dad's car on the way home. Older brother uncles can usually be relied on not to resort to this kind of trick.[1] In fact, it's usually the other way round. It's your dad trying to get his kids sick! This is particularly the case if the older brother uncle has made more of his life than your mum or dad have. Nothing pulls a family apart (and spoils Christmas) quicker than a spot of brotherly jealousy!

Catch Phrase

I've got an idea – let's see if we can eat a burger, fries and shake on the "Corkscrew". You ought to see it coming, but you won't. This is your uncle's way of saying *I'm jealous of your dad's new car!*

Avoidance Tactics

Have a word with your cousins. After all, they're your uncle's children, so they're probably used to dodging him on a regular basis!

---

1. But don't bank on it!

Very Distant Relative .... 🏃

By very distant I'm not referring to some relative who lives a long way away, although this particular species often does. I'm talking about someone who isn't a close relative like a brother.

Relationship

They could be second cousin, third cousin once removed, etc., and belong to some obscure branch of the family that you only ever see at funerals, and only then if there's money involved!

Habitat

It's hard to say. They could live under a stone for all anyone knows. Certainly they often look as though they might.

Behaviour

Strange. This is what makes them appealing to the younger members of the family. They seem to have lived a fascinating life, according to the tales they tell. Of course, most of these are made up. They actually work in a library. This should be obvious from the way they look and dress, the cobwebs behind their ears, etc. Let's face it – they don't look anything like someone who hang-glides off the top of Mount Everest before breakfast. They're on a Zimmer frame for a start.[1]

---

1. Even the scantiest knowledge of geography should have told you that the Everest tale was a non-starter. He lives in Chelmsford!

Catch Phrase

Did I tell you about the time I . . . They say this just before launching into another implausible tale of single-handedly performing the impossible.[1]

Did she mention the money I lent her? This is usually said on being told that a particular relative has died. After they've spent hours convincing you that they're actually related to the dead person, that is.

Avoidance Tactics...

Pretend to be out when they call. If they phone, pretend to be an answering machine. Never make the mistake of pretending to be a Chinese laundry, just in case they can actually speak Cantonese and haven't made that up. In fact, go to whatever lengths are necessary to avoid this particular family member. "Why?" I hear you squeak. "They seem harmless enough." Ah, yes! And very amusing too. But just wait till they persuade your parents to let them move in because they're being pursued by the Welsh Intelligence Service. They won't leave till they're carried out in a box. And when they are, your poor parents will be left with a huge mountain of unanswered questions, not to mention an even huger mountain of unpaid bills!

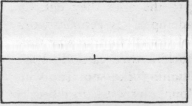

DISTANT RELATIVE

CLOSE RELATIVE

1. Sometimes literally single-handedly. Like the time they wrestled sixteen crocodiles with one arm tied behind their back. And they would have won if the crocs hadn't cheated!

Wife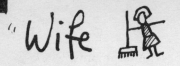

Having talked about husbands, it's only fair to mention wives. Not that any of you are either at the moment, but you may be one day, so it's as well to know what to expect!

Relationship

A wife is the woman married to a husband. She could be your mum. He could be your dad.

Habitat

This species is often found in the kitchen, or one pace behind a moving vacuum cleaner. However, don't make the mistake of thinking that this is their natural habitat, because it isn't. But cooking and housework are essential parts of running a home, whether we enjoy them or not. It's true, of course, that some women – and some men – take to it like a duck to water, but most of us would rather be a fish.

Behaviour

There's an old saying that goes "A woman's work is never done." Now this does not mean that women never finish anything, but rather that there's so much work involved in running a home that nobody, not even a woman, could get it all done, even if they didn't stop to watch *Home and Away*. Of course, this old saying presupposes that running a home is in some way *women's work*. But we know better, don't we? Or if we don't, we should. Because anything to do with the running of a home is the responsibility of everyone who lives in it. Oh, yeah, so it might fall to the woman of the house to crack the whip occasionally and make sure things get done (*see* Mothers), but that doesn't mean it's her *job*, does it? Anyway, she might already have a job, thank you very much. A very good job, which pays well and is a lot more rewarding than housework.[1] However, you'd be amazed at the number of men (and women) who still believe it's the wife's job to run the home. Try this simple test: point to any cupboard in your kitchen and ask your dad what's in it. He'll get as far as "String . . ." and give up.[2] Either that or he'll assume it's something to do with a school project and say: "I'm not helping you with your homework!" But the truth is probably that deep down he honestly believes it's nothing to do with him, because he's out at work all day and his wife (your mum) takes care of "that side of things". He conveniently forgets that she's probably out at work as well. And anyway, why should she be any better at it

---

1. Pretty well *anything* is more rewarding than housework. Except perhaps fishing.
2. And even then he'll be wrong, because hardly any homes have a useful bit of string knocking about. Sadly, this valuable commodity is under-rated these days.

than he is? She hasn't had any special training, has she? OK, so her mum might have passed on a few useful tips and a recipe for bread pudding, but that hardly makes her an expert, does it? In fact the sudden change from being single to being married comes as a shock to many a young woman. One minute she's a single, carefree girl, then, one marriage, one wedding reception with disco and four attempts to get her Uncle Ray to put his trousers back on and stop frightening the bridesmaids later, she's a wife! Mind you, it can be just as scary for the man. One minute he's a happy-go-lucky bachelor in

a bedsit, living on Cup-a-soup (Batchelor's, naturally!), then, one silly stag party, a night in a police cell, and six dozen blurred photos of relatives he's never met later, he's a husband! (See Husband.) No, it can't be easy for either of them. But what makes it harder for the wife is that her husband has probably had his mum running round after him, and it often takes a while for him to realise that his wife is *not* a replacement mum.

Catch Phrase

The washing-up needs doing. This is the sort of thing a wife might be tempted to say, particularly when she's a newly-wed. Usually it's a gentle hint that she's fed up with always getting lumbered with the dirty pots and pans. Of course, some husbands don't need a hint. They're in there with their sleeves rolled up before she can say "Watch that water – it's boiling!", which is a pity because sitting in a hospital casualty department for half the night with third-degree burns can really take the romance out of a relationship. Some wives try the more direct approach. They say: *Would you like to do the washing-up?* What they actually mean is, *Would you like me to teach you* how *to do the washing-up?* However, they won't really take "no" for an answer. Not even if you say "No, thank you."

Avoidance Tactics...

Well, the only way a man can avoid the worse excesses of a wife is not to get married, which does seem a bit drastic, particularly if he wants to. Alternatively, the way to avoid such strife is for the man to continue to treat his wife in the same way he treated her before they got married, when he was still trying to impress her!

X-Relative

This is what relatives become if they're involved in that most complex of situations, divorce.[1] A husband and wife split up and ripples run through the whole family, sometimes affecting dozens of innocent by-standing relatives. In-laws become out-laws. Mother-in-laws go back to being mothers, and their children (the x-wives and x-husbands) often go back to living with them. Relatives who have never given either partner the time of day suddenly start giving their advice, and everybody tries to work out whose fault it is. The fact is that it is rarely any one person's fault. These things happen. Unfortunately, the children of the marriage often imagine for some strange reason that it's their fault in some way. It never is. Never ever. So there!

1. Not always. It's possible for divorces to be very civilised affairs.

Younger Brother

Relationship

As with an older brother, a younger brother is someone who is male and has the same parents as you. The difference between this species and the older version is that a younger brother is obviously younger than you are. But this is far from being the only difference.

Habitat

Imagine the situation: you and a few of your mates are sitting around at home doing nothing in particular. Certainly nothing illegal.[1] Suddenly the room is invaded by a creature from the Planet Mudblob. What do you do? Call the police? Phone Patrick Moore? Say "OK, OK. Take me to your leader"? No. You just turn to your mates and say, "Don't worry. It's my little brother." Chances are they've got one of their own, so they won't be at all bothered.[2] So where else can you find younger brothers, apart from under piles of mud? The short answer is under anything else seriously unpleasant. Because that's what younger brothers are – seriously unpleasant. And for this reason they're attracted to anything seriously unpleasant from blocked drains to dead animals. If the drain's blocked by a dead animal, they're totally in their element.

1. Although by the time your younger brother has relayed it to your parents, it will be!
2. Do be careful though. I did hear of one poor lad who reacted in exactly the way described, only to discover that his bedroom had in fact been invaded by creatures from outer space. What his reaction was exactly I can't say, because he hasn't been seen since. Still, at least they didn't take his little brother with them as well, so in that way he must feel a certain sense of escape. If I was any kind of a writer I would now furnish you with a simple test for telling the difference between space aliens and younger brothers. Well, I would, but unfortunately no such test exists.

Behaviour

You might imagine that their need to delve into disgusting things is due to some inbuilt curiosity. Possibly you were helped towards this conclusion by the fact that little bro once took the cat apart to see how it worked. But you'd be wrong! Their need to coat themselves in anything unpleasant is some kind of animal instinct that goes with being a younger brother. Most of them grow up and out of it almost overnight. Those who don't grow out of it don't grow up much either, but find themselves attracted to jobs where there's a good chance of getting pelted with rotten food.[1] But why, given their obsession with filth, do they always want to come into the bathroom just when you're trying to get ready for that heavy date? For you guys, it's Her in 4b, isn't it? Let's face it, it's taken you two terms to pluck up the courage to ask your best mate to ask her out for you, and you don't want to blow it now. There you are in front of the mirror, trying to resolve the burning question:[2] will she go for the George Michael look or should you borrow your mum's tweezers and pluck both of those stray hairs out? For you girls it's Him in the fifth form, isn't it? He's been giving you these looks, hasn't he? It got so bad that you thought he might have a squint. But he didn't. He was trying to tell you with his eyes what his heart was feeling but his mind was too nervous to let his mouth try to put into words. With good reason, because the only time he tried to ask you out he got so tongue-tied you thought he was a Russian spy. Thank heavens for your best friend. OK, so she kept him for herself for three months, but she did eventually deliver his note, and now you're preparing for your first date.

1. Yes, John Major, our very own Prime Minister, is a grown-up younger brother!
2. Actually the burning starts when you splash the after-shave on!

You check through the cabinet for the smell that'll knock him sideways. You try out a few of your mum's and realise why Dad calls her the Pig Farmer. And all this time, what is little brother doing? Battering on the door and yelling, "Let me in or I'll do it in my pants!" This surprises you. After all, that's never bothered him in the past. He must be growing up!

Catch Phrase

I'm going to tell. This catch phrase strikes fear into the heart of the toughest. Mainly because you can never be sure *who* he's going to tell, and *what* he's going to tell them! Because, let's face it, all of us have at one time or another fallen into the trap of telling our little brother our innermost secrets. Oops! Mistake!

Avoidance Tactics...

You can't really avoid younger brothers. However, if the going gets really tough, just remember these simple facts:

1 Your brother will probably eventually get married.
2 He will then have children of his own, more than likely.
3 Because he's your brother, you'll be an aunt or uncle to his children.
4 Revenge is sweet![1]

---

1. This also applies to older brothers.

Younger Sister –

Relationship

Well, obviously she's your younger sister!

Habitat

Younger sisters can be found almost anywhere, usually where you don't want them. Rather like younger brothers, they take an unhealthy interest in your love life, such as it is. In fact they take an unhealthy interest in absolutely anything you want to keep private!

Behaviour

Unhealthy is the word! Although they're not as disgusting as younger brothers,[1] they're more embarrassing! They seem to know your innermost secrets and think nothing of spilling the beans. What's more, they choose the worst possible time, like when the vicar's dropped round. Of course, they're capable of keeping a secret at a price. And what a price! Unlike the younger brother who'll blurt out the secret after a few hours, his female counterpart can keep the secret for ever, if the right deal's been struck.[2] I suppose this is some comfort, even though you've had to sell all your records, clothes, teeth, etc. to buy her off. Don't be fooled. All I said was that she *could* keep your secret for ever, not that she *would!* This is because she *won't*. She'll only keep it until telling everyone can cause the most trouble. So be warned!

1. No-one could be!
2. I've met younger sisters who could teach the Mafia a thing or two!

Catch Phrase

I bet Mum would be really interested to know that you . . . etc., etc. That's how it starts. And within hours you've organised about 78 paper rounds for yourself, as well as setting up an odd-job service which you intend to try and fit in between shifts down the local coalmine.[1] Only by doing this will you keep her off your back!

Avoidance Tactics...

Impossible. After all, you live in the same house, don't you? That, plus the fact that your sweet little sister has inherited all your Mum's ninja creeping skills basically means that you're doomed.

Other Advice

The only way you can possibly hope to cope with this species is to persuade your mum and dad to have another little girl. That way your younger sister would have a younger sister of her own to cope with. But before you leap at this suggestion, check that there are no quads in your family first, otherwise you could be shooting yourself in the foot!

1. Do they still have one?

Zo......

that's the complete A–Z (or A–Y) of relatives. I'm sure I've missed some, but I think you'll find that pretty well every member of your family fits into one category or another. You may be thinking, "Great! Now I can handle them all!" Not at all. You see, as I have hinted throughout this book, many relatives behave differently when confronted by other relatives. So knowing how they react in isolation is only part of the picture. We also need to see how they respond in groups. Well, the best place to do that is at family functions: weddings, funerals, christenings, birthdays, getting-out-of-gaol parties, etc. This is when families let their hair down, take their toupees off and generally reveal themselves in their true colours. And frankly this can be a real eye-opener. Now naturally I can't reveal the goings-on at any of my family get-togethers, for fear of reprisals.[1] But, at great personal expense, I hired a team of hand-picked experts to do field work for me. Then I discovered that they were no good at picking strawberries, so I got them to work on this book instead. These experts were carefully selected for their ability to move among any gathering of relatives without arousing suspicion,[2] as well as for their cheapness. They were (and still are):

---

1. A couple of my uncles have already got a contract out on me.
2. Or arousing any unnatural passions in those present. To this end all my experts – to a man (and woman) – were extremely ugly. However, this didn't prevent one of them getting attacked by an amorous family pet.

Mike ("Mad Flasher") Jenkins

As the name suggests, Mike Jenkins is a photographer. He currently holds the record for wasting more rolls of film than anyone.[1] It's not that he's a bad photographer, as far as anyone knows. It's just that he insists on developing all his own prints. At home. In the bath. While he's in it (at the tap end). Of course this is no good for the photos, but it's given Mike a lovely matte finish. I wasn't going to have him on my team, but a set of snaps he took of me (with a telephoto lens) quickly persuaded me that he was exactly the sort of researcher I needed. After all, he could move unnoticed among the groups of relatives, partly in his capacity as a wedding photographer, but mainly due to his total lack of personality.[2]

Mildred Thrusscott

One of Mildred's great strengths is her ability to look like everyone's favourite aunt. Her other great strength is her ability to tear telephone directories in half. Such shows of muscle came in handy whenever anyone confronted her, saying: "Hang on! You're not my Auntie Doreen!" A couple

1. Including Lord Litchfield.
2. In fact it's possible to sit in a room with Mike and (as long as he doesn't speak) start to feel quite lonely. Of course if he *does* speak, you wonder where the noise is coming from.

of swift armlocks later the challenger was introducing her around the room as though they'd known her all their life. This knack of quickly becoming the life, soul and cabaret at any party made her a great asset. Also, being an aunt in her own right made her a few quid, since she was able to take orders for jumpers.

"Snotty" Johnstone

"Snotty" was the youngest human member of my team.[1] As a typical runny-nosed brat he was able to dash about, roll in the trifle, set fire to things and generally cause mayhem without anyone giving him a second thought. This didn't bother him, but he would soon have kicked up a fuss if they hadn't given him a second helping! "Snotty" could infiltrate any group of kids. Presumably they just assumed he was the cousin they didn't know they had. Anyway, any doubts they may have had were quickly forgotten when he revealed his patent method of making gunpowder out of two portions of jam roly-poly and an Eccles cake.

1. I'm assuming he *was* human. I didn't get that close.

Elderado Dingbatti

Of course no project of mine would be complete without Elderado on my team. He wouldn't have been a great deal of use, except for his uncanny ability to convince gullible people of his credentials. I say that (a) because he *does* have this ability, and (b) because he refused to let me use the term "con artist". Either way, Elderado wove his magical, if rather confused, way into the hearts and bosoms of many families. He even confided in me that, during this period of research, he had a proposal of marriage. He gave me all the details, and I must say it nearly broke my heart to see the tears coursing down his silicon cheeks[1] as I gently pointed out that he wouldn't be allowed to marry a sideboard, not even by special licence.

The Great Marvello and Daphne

Great and Daff (as they like to be called) are no strangers to families. They have spent many happy hours in other people's homes, firstly as cat burglars, but more recently as entertainers.[2] Veterans of the children's party circuit, they have turned balloon modelling into a complete waste of time. However, they were good as a distraction,[3] which made them very useful members of the

1. Having spent years in institutions has brought him into contact with many plastic surgeons, and Elderado has never been one to waste an opportunity. Sadly, it is largely due to plastic surgery that he has personality problems. When he looks in the mirror, he thinks he's somebody else!
2. People who have seen their act say that it's hard to spot the change of career. Either way they're an expensive intrusion.
3. In fact some people became so distracted watching their act that they had to be sedated.

team. In fact there was only one occasion when I even vaguely regretted using them. This was a birthday party. Great was halfway through a particularly tricky ... er ... trick when "Snotty" Johnstone, who was one of the invited guests, yelled out: "I know how that's done!"[1] I tactfully whispered to "Snotty" that Great and Daff were part of my team. Unfortunately it only made matters worse. But Great was a trouper. He rose above it. Or rather "Snotty" rose above it. Great levitated him and left him stuck to the ceiling. He was very resourceful, I must say.

Dave the Hamster

Not everyone's idea of a great conversationalist, but Dave's a great talking point, due largely to his unusual – and unsavoury – habits, none of which we need to go into here. Suffice it to say, whenever I needed a hamster (which was never), Dave was there. What a trouper! What an eater! What a disgusting animal! But, since pets play an important role in family life, I thought it wise to have him on board. It wasn't. Quite the reverse in fact. But more of Dave later.

1. Which, actually, was more than the Great Marvello did, judging from his performance.

Well, that's the team. And now the assignment. As you know, I had previously decided that the only real way to observe families in their natural environment, as it were, was to infiltrate various family gatherings. As I've said, relatives only behave naturally when they're in close proximity to their nearest and dearest. (Well, the rest of the family, anyway!) But where to start? Where would we find unsuspecting human guinea-pigs for us to observe? Well, the best place to find out who's getting married, born or has just died is the local paper. So we clubbed together and bought one. And at last we were on the first rung of a ladder that would eventually lead us into the hearts and minds of a number of total strangers' families! The fruits of our labours are now revealed for all to see.

Births, Deaths, Marriages and Fights

Flick through any newspaper[1] and although you won't find anything that's true, you'll probably find a Births, Marriages and Deaths column. Of course it may be separate columns. I mean to say, it's very unlikely that a birth, marriage and death would all take place at the same time in the same family, although this isn't impossible. Our research turned up the following oddity in a local paper:

There was a bit of a stir today at the church of St Mildred in the Wardrobe with St Jude. Bride Chastity Huggins, 19, collapsed at the altar and gave birth to a bouncing baby boy.[2] Groom Denis Tarvey, 22, was so overcome with shock that he also collapsed. Unfortunately, he did not give birth to a bouncing baby boy. He died. All was not lost, however, since the Reverend Dirk Truly, 49, offered to perform a wedding, funeral and christening all at the same time, half price, as long as a replacement could be found for the unfortunate late groom. A replacement was quickly found by means of a raffle with all proceeds going to the bride's father's favourite charity, the Pig and Whistle, *where a wedding reception took place later. The new groom, Denzil Shaver, 34, said, "I can't believe my luck! I've never won anything before in my life. What's her name again?"*

1. Actually, it's as quick to read some newspapers cover to cover as it is to flick through them!
2. It's just as well the baby was bouncing, because those stone church floors can be really hard.

Of course such things are extremely unusual. But if you do scan these columns you'll see various announcements, usually followed by a line of verse, an elegy, or an epigram, such as:

BIRTHS: *To Roger and Caroline McQueen, a bonny baby boy Billy McQueen. A brother for Christopher, Lucinda, Karl, Francis, Stephen and David. "Onto our lives a ray of sun doth fall."*

DEATHS: *Passed away quietly Tuesday morning (am): Frederick George Dangler. Leaves a wife and family. "Gone but not forgotten."*

MARRIAGES: *Mr and Mrs Hubert Tubby are pleased to announce the forthcoming marriage of their daughter Maureen to Lance Corporal Anthony (Tony) Tibbs. "At last!"*

These announcements always tell a story. Take the Dangler one, for instance. The following week the same newspaper printed a correction saying that although her husband was "gone but not forgotten", Mrs Dangler had however forgotten that his name was Reg and not Fred. Fred was the milkman's name.

A Wedding is Announced

The union of Tracy Wedge and Partridge Fester was the biggest affair that the village of Much Snoring had ever seen. Mainly because, due to a Local Authority blunder, the village had only just been declared safe from the Black Plague, which last raged there in 1357. Consequently it has always been difficult to get a decent crowd at any of the local church discos,[1] and totally impossible to hold a wedding reception. So the Wedge-Fester "do" was very much a first.[2]

1. Partly because of the Plague ruling, but mostly because the discos are rubbish.
2. And a last, as it turned out!

The thing about weddings is that everyone's on their best behaviour for the church part. I think this is actually why a lot of families hold their weddings in church.[1] It doesn't have a lot to do with religion. In fact the last time Tracy Wedge went to church the vicar dropped her in the font![2] Likewise, most of her family weren't great church-goers, but were even now arranged neatly on one side of the church. The Festers, all 45 of them, were packed into the pews opposite.

When the bride, groom, and immediate family retired to sign the register, giving the rest of the relatives a few minutes to eye each other up, the church organist, Mr Tiffly from the Co-op, struggled to play a medley of *Worlds Apart* hits. This was Tracy's choice. Unfortunately, she didn't take into account the musical ability of either Mr Tiffly or *Worlds Apart*. Consequently this musical delight was totally incomprehensible and far too short.

After that, it was outside for the photos. I had arranged for Mike Jenkins (one of my team) to take the snaps. This went quite well, once he'd managed to get the film in the camera, and fought off Tracy's uncle Reg, who saw himself as a bit of a photography buff and wanted to keep checking Mike's exposure. There was one nasty moment[3] when Mike, ever the master of tact, got everyone together for the big group shot and then said to Partridge, a little too loudly: "Bung the ones you can't stand on the ends, then you can cut 'em off later!"

I had had the foresight to send my lot (Mildred, "Snotty", Great, Daphne and Elderado[4]) on ahead. This

1. The fighting breaks out much earlier at Registry Office weddings.
2. He reminded her of this during the wedding ceremony, which was a bit embarrassing.
3. If you don't count Mike Jenkins eventually "nutting" Uncle Reg.
4. We didn't bother to take Dave the Hamster. We didn't think weddings would be his thing, somehow.

was a mistake, as the buffet lunch was already laid out. However, I managed to get the local pub to rustle up some replacement sandwiches, so I don't think too many of the guests noticed except Tracy, who turned out to be a vegetarian[1] when the pub could only do Spam. Elderado came to the rescue, cunningly disguised as a waiter,[2] and suggested that Tracy try the nouvelle cuisine sandwiches. Since she was on a diet (which wasn't working) she readily agreed. What could these sandwiches be? I asked myself, secretly fearing the answer. Yes, I was right! They were the Spam ones with the Spam taken out.

1. As well as a pain in the bum!
2. So cunningly disguised, in fact, that everyone thought he was an escaped lunatic. What probably gave him away was the waiter's uniform, which was quite clearly a doctor's coat bitten off at the waist.

Now, there's nothing like a family gathering to bring emotions to the fore, and this wedding was no exception. By the time the speeches came around Tracy's dad was very emotional and by the time he'd finished telling everyone how he couldn't stand Partridge, what a stupid name Partridge was anyway,[1] and he would never have let him marry his daughter if they hadn't needed the spare bedroom because Granny was coming to live with them, various assorted cousins had worked out how to get the wheels off Partridge's Audi (or the "getaway car" as Partridge had been referring to it all week). Getaway sledge now, more like! Of course this bit of harmless fun sparked off a revolution, or rather got Partridge's brother Noël a broken nose, and Tracy's sister Dulcie laddered tights.[2] Thus started a family feud. First came the blame:

"Well, don't look at me!" said the vicar, but Tracy's cousin Brian hit him anyway. Unable to decide exactly whose fault it was, they then moved on to the recriminations:

"If you hadn't done such and such, then he wouldn't have done such and such!"

"I never did such and such! What *is* such and such anyway?"

"Don't get clever with me!"

That did it! No-one had ever called Noël clever before, and he didn't like it. Soon punches were flying rather than words. The various aunts, washing up in the community hall kitchen, put down the plates and took

1. You may well have been thinking the same. Let me explain. Partridge's name is a monument to his mother's habit of giving birth near Christmas. His brother's called Noël and his sisters Holly and Ivy. Having been born on the first day of Christmas, Partridge was called Partridge. (It could have been worse. He could have been called Peartree, or Eightmaidsamilking!)
2. Though not, it has to be said, as a direct result of anything to do with the car! Well, not the Audi, anyway!

up cudgels.[1] At first they couldn't quite work out whose side to be on. After all, family loyalty's one thing, but they'd all suddenly remembered that they were sisters. So, as well as Wedge v Fester it was sister v sister, and in no time at all it was brother v brother in the car park, uncle v uncle in the Gents toilet (ditto aunts in the Ladies) and elderly aunt v elderly aunt – knitting needles at thirty paces – behind the wedding cake. The only place that was safe was the under-stairs cupboard, if you didn't mind sharing it with an assortment of grandads.

Battle raged until the four grannies sat down in the Bingo annex and ironed out their differences. There weren't any really except the fact that they all hated each other, but the grannies knew that anyway, and they were never going to sort that out! So all that remained was to round up their tribe, box a few ears, and go home. And that's what happened. Everyone went home and the car wheels went "walkies".

PLAY FAMILY FEUD (TM) CARD GAME
COMPLETE THE FAMILY PICTURE BY PAIRING THE RELATIVES

1. Well, cups of Fairy Liquid actually.

From that day, some members of the family never spoke to each other again, except to have the occasional conversation. Noël didn't speak to anyone at all for six weeks. He'd had his jaw wired. Great Aunt Gladys spoke to the vicar, got his measurements and made him a double-breasted cardigan in cable stitch.

And Tracy and Partridge, what of them? Well, they moved up to the North-east for a fresh, if blowy, start. But it didn't work out and they got a divorce. And so a marriage made in heaven ended in Hull. And did they ever find out whose idea it was to take the wheels of the Audi? I hear you ask. Well, even if you're not asking, I'll name the guilty party. Step forward one "Snotty" Johnstone, a lad who can always be relied upon to get things going. Was he responsible for ruining their lives? No, no! He saved them from themselves! He held up a metaphorical mirror, and let them see into their inner selves. He helped them to relive the hurt of their youth and finally to take revenge for all those moments of sibling cruelty. He made those aunts and uncles realise just what they had been put through as brothers and sisters. He made them retaliate. (Oh, and he also made twenty quid a piece on the wheels.)

Funerals

Funerals are just the same as weddings, but without the cake. By that I'm not suggesting that everyone gets roaring drunk and insults everyone else, although they might if they get the chance. No, funerals bring out different hidden qualities in relatives. They also bring out different relatives – relatives that you tend not to see at other functions. They don't usually bother with family weddings. They offer excuses like: "We'd have to travel thirty miles, and how could we be sure they'd still love each other by the time we got there?" Well, with 30

DID YOUR PARENTS COME HERE TO SHARE IN THE COLLECTIVE SORROW?

NO...THEY CAME HERE TO SHARE IN THE COLLECTING SILVER

per cent of all marriages ending in divorce,[1] they may have a point. But they're not at this funeral to discuss the lasting properties of love. Oh, no! They're there to discuss crockery. Family silver even, if there is any.

So it was on a bright August morning that I and my team bought Awaydays to Pleck in the West Midlands for the funeral of Nellie Jerkin (Mrs), late of this parish.

1. That's obviously just a rough estimate, because 50 per cent of my marriages ended in divorce!

Pleck is every bit as awful as it sounds. Don't be impressed by the fact that it has a wine château there.[1] This is actually a Dubonnet bottling plant. But I have to say that it's the perfect place for a funeral, even in summer. You couldn't imagine anyone spoiling the solemnity of the occasion by suddenly smiling for no reason. In fact our contact up there, Greg Starling of the *Walsall Observer* newspaper, told us that a local by-law prevented smiling without good reason, on pain of being made to live in the area for the rest of your life.

Anyway, the service at the crematorium went without a hitch. None of the Jerkin family children were there.

1. Imaginatively called Château Pleck.

They'd been barred from such occasions ever since young Trev[1] tried to organise an impromptu barbecue. The Reverend Tasker, presiding, made a lovely speech about Nellie, reminding everyone present what a brilliant footballer she was until a cartilage injury put her out of the game. He went on to relive that marvellous moment when she scored with a header outside the box in the 1935 FA Cup, the one and only time Walsall have played in the Cup. It was about then that Uncle Norman, whose pacemaker had just woken him up by shorting, pointed out that the vicar had got her muddled up with somebody else. She had never ever played football at Club level, not even as a joke.

Cousin Winnie wanted to have the lid off the coffin, just to make sure they'd got the right body. She became most insistent. It turned out that she was more concerned that Nellie might not be dead at all, because she'd got her eye on a nice matching pair of silver candlesticks. Anyway, she was eventually persuaded to put the crowbar back in her handbag, and the ceremony continued. Then it was back to the house, where Auntie Brenda, Barrie's second wife on Big Nan's side, was cutting the crusts off the sandwiches and baby-sitting the family children.[2]

Seeing the family crammed into Nellie's terraced house really put them in perspective. There they were, all arranged in order of grief. The conversation about poor Nellie herself ran out at about the same time as the sandwiches did.[3] The vicar had said it all, even though none of it was true. The children had taken her collec-

1. Who was now twenty-seven.
2. Well, guarding the key to the coal shed, actually, in case anyone used it to let the kids out.
3. Sandwiches which "Snotty" had offered to chew for anyone who hadn't got their own teeth.

tion of walking sticks into the back garden and were having a macabre and impromptu game of hockey, using a ball of Great Aunt Agatha's wool.

The pleasantries over, a heavy silence descended, broken only by the after-effects of too many cucumber sandwiches, and the squeaky voice of Great-Great-Aunt Faith, who kept saying "Who's dead again?" Throughout this the collective eyes of the family started drifting around the rooms, alighting on anything of possible value. And then it started. Uncle Denis, ever the subtle one, suddenly pointed to a fading picture on the wall that looked like it might be worth a bob or two[1] and exclaimed: "Oh, *that's* where I left my original Picasso! On Nellie's wall! I was wondering what I'd done with it!" The fact that he hadn't been near the old girl since he was three was irrelevant; he quickly slipped it off the wall and into the boot of his Metro before you could say "grave robber".

Never slow to catch on, the rest of the family started playing the same game. Soon the room looked a bit like the floor of the Stock Exchange and the air was filled with cries of: "There's that 47-piece dinner service Nellie always wanted me to have!" and "None of you will know this because Nellie said that it should be our little secret, but she promised me all her jewellery."

Soon the relatives were vying for the same items. And they were using the only weapon left to them – a weapon relatives always use when the chips are down. The past. What happened when they were children:

"Nellie always liked you better than me! I should

1. The painting might be worth a bob or two, I mean. Not the wall! Although, ironically, when Denis got the thing home and had it valued he might as well have been talking about the wall – or even just the wallpaper!

never have taken the blame when you tinkled on her prize aspidistra and killed it!"

"Rubbish! She liked me better because I *am* better!"

"Better than what? A slug?"

"Say that again if you dare!"

"Who's dead again?"

Even the children abandoned their game of hockey,[1] and came rushing into the house to see what all the fuss was about. It got so embarrassing that Great and Daff offered to "take the kiddies into another room and do a magic show". But the children wanted none of it. They wanted to see Aunt Maud's brilliant left hook again. It had caught Uncle Frank right under the jaw and sent him scuttling into the 47- (now 3456-) piece dinner service. Those kids had never seen anything like it! Grown adults behaving just like spoilt children. After Greg Starling had got a few decent photos for the paper by staging a few action replays, we made our excuses and left.

Travelling back on the train we were all rather quiet, mainly because we had seen the past lives of total strangers unroll before our eyes. And they were horribly like our own.

In a desperate attempt to cheer us all up, Mildred Trusscott suggested that maybe this was not typical. We reminded her that the wedding had gone pretty well the same way. Undaunted, she suggested that we should withhold judgment until we had all the facts. After all, we were going to a christening in Reading the very next day. Surely the nature of such a joyous occasion was bound to bring out the best in a family, wasn't it?

1. Which had since degenerated into a game of "Let's knock the heads off the flowers with these walking sticks. Aunty Nellie will never know!"

Christenings

There's nothing quite like a christening to make a family look their best. Ribbons, bibbons, frills and lace, and that's just the blokes! Weddings are a great occasion for dressing up, of course, but they can get out of hand. A christening is a far more contained and ordered occasion. This must be due to some degree to the nature of the event. A christening is the acceptance of a new life into the family of God.[1] It is both a joyous and a solemn occasion. That's the theory, anyway!

You see, the problems with christenings actually start way back before the actual event. They really start with the birth of the child, and go downhill from there. The first problem is what to call the baby. Its parents might consider using the name of various relatives, however hideous.[2] If it's a girl, should it be named after the mother, the mother's mother, the father's mother, the

1. Naturally other religions have similar ceremonies, too numerous to detail here. Therefore I've concentrated on the one I know most about!
2. The names as well as the relatives.

mother's mother's mother, the father's mother's mother, the mother's mother's mother's sister, the father's mother's mother's brother . . . ooops! Sorry! Even I got confused there. But you can see the problem, can't you? You can name the child after one relative and offend others, or you can name it after a different relative and offend different others, or you can name it after nobody at all, and offend everybody! The choice is yours. This is often why the christening doesn't happen immediately. The new parents are waiting until all the fuss about the baby's names has died down before they announce who the Godparents will be and start another row!

I've never really understood the point of having relatives as Godparents. After all, they're going to look after the child's welfare anyway, aren't they?[1] What's the point of giving them the same job twice? Because, after all, that's basically what Godparents are all about, in this day and age. The other Godparental duty of making sure that the child is brought up in the Christian faith is a harder one to enforce. What do you do? Phone the kid up and ask him if he's going to church? Yes, probably.

Anyway, having survived the flak over names and choice of Godparents, the parents then set a date for the christening, happily believing that they've got away with it all. They haven't. Come the big day, the knives will be out. The auntie who believed that the child should have been named after her, even though it's a boy, will present the baby with a lovely knitted cardigan, with the comment: "Oh, dear! I made it as big as I could without buying up the entire wool shop. But it looks like it might be too small for him. Still, he *is* rather a chubby little chap, isn't he? Rather like his mum and dad!" Ouch!

1. In theory, anyway.

Then the uncle who wanted to be a Godparent because he mistakenly believed that you got paid for it, gives the "Little Nipper" a money box.

"Not that he'll need it! You two will have spent any cash he gets before he can put it in there!" Double ouch!

And so it goes on. Should one of the parents decide to confront any of these disgruntled relatives, all the old hurts and childhood slights will come out.

"Your kid's only fat because you are! And you're only fat because you used to pinch my breakfast when I was little and couldn't defend myself![1]

Is there any logic in that? Is stealing a baby's food when you're seven going to make you fat when you're twenty-four? Unlikely, I'd say. Mind you, to me all baby food looks as if it's more likely to make you throw up than get fat. But that won't stop some grown-up sister or brother throwing it in your face.[2]

All these thoughts came up over a cup of instant cocoa in the Dunnsleepininahalfdecentbed Guest House and Palsey Clinic, just outside Reading. In fact, as a result of this discussion, the team and I decided that we really couldn't face going and watching young Sharon Louise Harold Endercott[3] having water splashed in her face the following morning. We decided we couldn't face going back to a stranger's house in a stranger's car to eat even stranger fishpaste sandwiches and watch them cut the christening cake with the same knife they had used to cut the atmosphere.

So we decided to give the christening a miss and gatecrash a pools-winner party instead. Some lucky devil

---

1. I'm here to tell you that the particular aunt who made that comment has never been that little.
2. Not the food itself, but the fact that you stole it. Although most brothers and sisters I know aren't above hurling baby food at each other.
3. Named after all the relevant relatives, poor thing!

had come up on the football pools and was throwing a bit of a party for his intimate circle of best friends. Naturally they'd had to hire the biggest hall in the area! So we went along because, as Elderado put it in a rare moment of lucidity, at least you can be sure everyone's there for the right reason! Sometimes I think he might be brighter than he looks![1] Ironically, we were later joined by most of the christening party, who turned out to be life-long friends of the chap who'd won the pools, whichever one he was!

And Finally..

Well, that's it. We've reached the end of another long and bumpy journey through other people's lives. I hope you found it useful in your fight to stay sane among your own relatives. One final piece of advice. You won't go far wrong if you remember this simple maxim:
BLOOD IS THICKER THAN WATER, BUT SOME RELATIVES ARE THICKER THAN BOTH OF THEM!
Happy coping with the family!

1. Oh, he must be! Nobody could be that stupid!

Afterword

One of the worst things about having brothers and sisters is hand-me-downs. After all, who wants to walk around in something that made dogs follow your brother down the street? I certainly don't, and I don't even know your brother! The trouble is that clothes go out of fashion so quickly that even your elder brother/sister wouldn't be seen dead in them, even if they fitted. Not that this latest garment you've "inherited" fits you, but your mum keeps saying you'll grow into it. How can you possibly grow into it when you're cringing with embarrassment? But all parents do this, don't they? They even *buy* things too big for you, so that they'll last longer. Or perhaps they're buying them for you but secretly thinking they could let your older brother/sister wear them for a bit until you're taller. That way they'll get the most wear out of them. Well, I can tell them how to get the most wear out of things – leave them in the shop till they fit the person they're intended for!

Some parents are so devious that they give your older brother's clothes to Oxfam, then go and buy them back for you! And they think you won't notice! They must realise you're not that stupid, even though you're related to them! They must also realise that you don't want to wear your older brother's/sister's clothes. After all, your mum was your age once and had to do the same. Doesn't your auntie keep reminding her of this?

Anyway, this book isn't a hand-me-down. So if any of your relatives fancy a shufty at it, tell them to get their own. Because if you do let them read it, they'll probably find themselves revealed in these pages, and they won't like what they see!